Swing Symphony

ANOTHER MIDLIFE ADVENTURE IN THE SOUTH OF FRANCE

Christopher Lawrence

KNOPF

A Knopf book
Published by Random House Australia Pty Ltd
20 Alfred Street, Milsons Point, NSW 2061
http://www.randomhouse.com.au

Sydney   New York   Toronto
London   Auckland   Johannesburg

First published in 2004
Copyright © Christopher Lawrence 2004
Illustration © Pete Poplaski 2004

National Library of Australia
Cataloguing-in-Publication Entry

Lawrence, Christopher.
Swing Symphony: another midlife adventure in the south of France.

ISBN 1 74051 210 3.

1. Lawrence, Christopher. 2. Swing (Music). 3. Languedoc
(France) – Social life and customs. 4. Languedoc (France) –
Description and travel. I. Title.

914.483

Cover image by Getty Images
Cover design by Sabine Pick
Internal design by Anna Warren, Warren Ventures
Typeset by Midland Typesetters, Maryborough, Victoria
Printed and bound by Tien Wah Press, Singapore

10 9 8 7 6 5 4 3 2 1

For Ian Kortlang and Claire Montgomery

CONTENTS

FRENESI

ARTIE SHAW AND HIS ORCHESTRA, HOLLYWOOD, 1940

It was fiesta down in Mexico
And so I stopped a while to see the show
I knew that frenesi
Meant 'Please love me'
And I could say frenesi

O KAY, SO IT ISN'T SHAKESPEARE. Or Alan Jay Lerner, for that matter. But I'm a sucker for a song lyric that sits happily in a puddle of simply rendered cliché. For one thing, it's easy to remember once you're over forty. No decoding is required; the escapist whimsy sits there as happily as your mother's cupcake.

The tune of *Frenesi* has every reason to be playing in my mental jukebox on this warm spring morning. It is the start of a holiday. The flowers lining the village streets seem to nod their heads in time with the passing street band. And while the music isn't mariachi, there is a distinctly Latin preponderance of cornets. Hang on – these flowers really *are* nodding their heads. Some take off abruptly atop spindly legs from their kerbside positions and head for the steps of the town hall to prepare for the 'prettiest flower' judging. Closer inspection reveals them to be children in costume. An old woman is nearly stampeded in a tide of impatient petals.

Stirred by the tang of brass in the air, the sun turns into a beautician, applying a touch of luminous rouge to the austere faces of nearby houses. There are some red cheeks on the faces of those swarming through the *place* as well. I have dodged the solar makeover by sandwiching myself between the Café du Commerce's awning and a beer. After several draughts I feel as if I am inside a sentimental song and that everyone around me knows the tune. In such an ambience, the likelihood of forming a friendship with the stranger at the next table is not merely possible, but imminent. With a pang of guilt mixed with regret, I imagine this is what a sense of community feels like.

A black blur appears suddenly between open windows, followed by a flamenco-like click of boot heels landing on the paved street, and . . . *voilà!* He stands before me, a living exclamation mark: Zorro, poised in fighting stance, *épée* glinting in the morning sun.

Dark eyes flash recognition from behind the famous mask. 'Hey, *amigo,*' he says, 'you wanna have a coffee later at the Jardin?'

'Sure, Pete,' I reply.

Doubtless I will have to pay if Pete is issuing the invitation. He may well be the world authority on the fictional swordsman, the owner of a burgeoning collection of Zorro memorabilia, but this passion provides only a meagre living. In this particular village, and with just a little help from some particular friends, meagre is enough.

With a swirl of his cape, the dark apparition turns, resheaths his sword and swaggers away across the square through clusters of two-legged bouquets, pausing only to restore the old woman to her tenuous upright stance. Poor thing, I think while sipping benevolence from the sparkling air, she's been attacked by flowers and rescued by a Mexican crime fighter and it's not even lunchtime. No wonder she looks confused.

Ordinarily the sight of Zorro in a village square would turn a few heads, even in Mexico. But not here. This isn't Mexico. The quasi-mariachi music reveals itself to be the old march *Sambre et Meuse*. Those two-legged flowers are *coquelicots*. A woman at the next table, who may soon be my friend if the gestures I use to punctuate my shabby vocabulary are sufficiently vivid, is crunching a croissant. There are several berets on older heads in the distance. And – more penetrating than the proud discordance of the brass band now pushing its wall of sound towards the *mairie*, more indicative than the catalogue of languages coursing around me, or the unfailing optimism of chiming bells, or the birds swirling above the festivities like confetti – it is the smoke of a thousand Gauloises that makes the pungent proclamation: I am in the south of France on a May day. To be more precise – and to give the situation all the resonance of a simple song like *Frenesi* – I am in a medieval village in the Gard, surrounded by carousing locals.

Who cares about *Frenesi*'s words, anyway? For those old enough to remember, *Frenesi* is the tune that swings from Artie Shaw's clarinet in the hit recording he made on March 3rd, 1940. The arrangement seduces from the start, gentle strings undulating like warm air. Artie's first few bars are almost decorous, but within seconds he starts to play just a little fast and loose with the melody, changing the features of a friend we've only just met.

Yet the whole effect is as neat as a pin. Like all great seductions, this one has been meticulously planned and well rehearsed. Artie Shaw's *Frenesi* is as precise as classical chamber music, not least because the arrangement was made by William Grant Still (1895–1978), an Afro-American composer who was more at home writing in classical forms like symphonies and operas, despite picking up some coin early in his career as a dance-band player.

There is none of your small swing band here. This is closer to an orchestra, combining strings, woodwind and tight brass, something grander and more conventionally glamorous. It is a groundbreaking example of what we now call crossover, and what a crossing it is: an American of Russian/Jewish descent who mastered a style derived from black music, and a Mexican love song arranged by a black classical composer. This mélange of musicians and styles from the USA's demographic margins combined to make a mainstream hit. *That* was the exciting story of jazz and swing in those days, when people unwittingly left open the doors of their taste and were surprised by the way the furniture was rearranged in the turbulence of the unexpected and strangely scented wind. People still love that music, still breathe that wind, as a tonic, for the liberating force of its rhythm, the attractive fragrance of its exotica, its loose fun. But underneath the surface of skittish riffs alluding to a condition of casual disarray, I suspect there lay a summons to a life on the rocks.

My life had entered its own rocky scenario – indeed, this French village is lapped on one side by the so-called Mer des Rochers (Sea of Rocks) – and so, too, did Artie Shaw's, over and over. Never one to remain content with the furniture, or the wife he shared it with, Artie made an art form of disillusionment. Born in 1910 and a professional musician by his teens, he threw the game away in 1933 to chop wood and read books in a remote Pennsylvanian farmhouse. A year later, he was back doing session work in New York City, and by the decade's end he had briefly usurped Benny Goodman as the 'King of Swing', having helped to push the genre into the popular mainstream with a 1936 concert at Broadway's Imperial Theatre and early recorded hits like *Begin The Beguine*. The clarinettist/bandleader progressed from cult figure to international icon. By 1941, *Time* magazine reported that the USA's image to warmongering Germans was comprised of 'skyscrapers, Clark Gable and Artie Shaw'.

Two years before this, Shaw had decamped again, walking out on both his renowned band and the music business to escape to Mexico in something of a *frenesi*. It is a recurring theme in Shaw's life. As soon as he suspected he was in a box – whether it was the threat of an ongoing career as a successful artist, a band that was on a roll, or a marriage (in total, two wives more than Henry VIII) – he wasted no time in stepping right outside it. This ambivalence about almost everything is charted in verbose detail in his 1953 autobiography *The Trouble with Cinderella*, published at the same time that Shaw hung up his clarinet for good and relocated to a cliff-top house in Spain.

My little table at the Commerce has become something of a drop-in centre after Zorro's departure. Johnny Weissmuller Jnr limps through the maze of clientele, rasping his *bonjours* in an almost inaudible smoker's voice, crushing every hand in a vice-like grip. The Artist, his aura of fragility taut as a bubble, nervously takes a nearby table and nurses a sauvignon blanc while dabbing away at his latest impressions of the village as seen from the Pont Vieux.

The Maestro comes over to remind me of the following night's rehearsal of the local choir, warning that our vocal resources have been dramatically weakened by the sudden departure of Ivan the bass for unspecified 'personal' reasons. She relates this bad news in a matter-of-fact tone, being accustomed to sudden departures after the precedent set by her former husband. Unreliability is the choir's anthem; one that we might sing if most of the members could be bothered to turn up each week. I am often the only tenor, and now, with

Ivan having scarpered and the Artist frequently indisposed, am likely to become the only bass as well.

It seems to be a cardinal rule of sleepy places that people are never so preoccupied as when they have nothing else to do. Many here are too 'busy' to be relied upon. What actually *keeps* them busy in this crucible of indolence is harder to explain. But no doubt we will all come up with something . . . tomorrow. Zorro may be our only hope.

Immured in thoughts of tessitura, I barely hear the scrape of my table's other chair above the surrounding cacophony of languages, brass band and the *clunk!* of the café's shallow metal ashtrays as they are wiped and replaced. Booker has shrugged off the previous night's excesses and emerged from his apartment into the morning, smooth-faced as ever and wearing a festive cravat. He relaxes his hands in his lap, instantly creating the impression he has been seated for a considerable time.

'*Hello to you,*' he murmurs in a George Sanders voice, his standard form of greeting. Its theatricality suits this carnival setting.

We exchange pleasantries and resume our musical observations of the night before, when he unveiled the treasures from his latest assault on the *puces* at Alès, including a rare copy of *Women Will Rule The World* recorded in 1935 by 'Attila the Hun' (aka Trinidadian calypso pioneer Raymond Quevedo).

'Just two euros,' Booker gloats. 'The guy there didn't know what he had. This is a precursor of rap; social comment in the vernacular of the street.'

The song is admittedly more a curio than a classic, and as poetry the lyric rates lower than *Frenesi*, even though Quevedo was revered as the 'Shakespeare of Calypso':

> *I'm offering a warning to men take care*
> *Of Modern Woman beware*
> *Even the flappers you cannot trust*
> *For they are taking our jobs from us*
> *And if you men don't assert control*
> *Women will rule the world*

Despite these portentous words, Attila doesn't sound too worried. Maybe it is the nickname, a rather aggressive one for a calypso singer. His band is so blissed out by late-night fatigue, Caribbean languor or a truckload of hooch they can barely play. The record is yet another eccentric addition to Booker's collection of more than 10,000 pieces of shellac – a number that is constantly on the rise with his bounty from regular raids on the weekly flea markets.

Our verbal ruminations on the likelihood of Attila making it as a songwriter in today's PC world are interrupted by the sight of Franceline the accordion virtuoso striding past a cluster of screaming sunflowers on the far side of the fountain. At this distance we are reminded that she possesses more than just musical skill. Her body type is custom designed to inspire Booker's friend and fellow shellac collector R. Crumb to reach for his pen: strong ankles, nothing reticent about her hips and buttocks, a wide and slightly gap-toothed smile. If Franceline could rule the world I suspect even Attila the Hun would have been happy.

But she is not smiling at us. Instead, her imperial sensuality is directed at a bald, tanned man standing outside the new real estate agent's window. He turns to receive her welcoming embrace; like her lucky accordion, he would appear to be her squeeze. This is news to me, for at an impromptu jam session chez Daniel last week Franceline was visibly enamoured with a more hirsute guitarist.

Booker notes my quizzical expression. 'Yes – it's over,' he explains. (A good jazz pianist, he is well positioned on the local musicians' grapevine.) 'Eric told me yesterday. He used to drive over to Franceline's twice a week for something steamy, but during his most recent visit he noticed a certain diminution of enthusiasm on her part. It only took the obvious question to prompt her. She announced that there was someone else.'

'Ouch. What did he do?'

'He was slightly nonplussed, as you can imagine. But she's

a good sport, Franceline. She offered him a farewell blowjob for old times' sake. He accepted, naturally.'

'So this is the new guy?'

'That's him. *Bruno.*' Booker drawls out the name, affecting an exaggerated sleaziness. 'The mysterious man of many parts. Most of them are in his workshop in Sète. He fixes her accordion.'

'Franceline has taken up with her *repairman*?' I struggle to keep my voice level, hoping to still a small pulse of cynicism.

There is a slight pause as we survey the increasingly tactile scene. 'At least they look happy,' Booker says. 'Still, one has to admit it is a highly cost-efficient move on her part.'

'Eric will get over it,' I surmise, having no idea as to whether Eric is about to throw himself into the Vidourle river, or smash his guitar against a tourist bus, but suspecting neither. And then, more as a tease than from a real desire to know, I offer the consolatory fantasy: 'I suppose he still has the others?'

'Oh yes,' muses Booker. 'He still has the others.'

Please love me. I sip my beer as Artie Shaw's *Frenesi* wells up in my head. That naff old lyric is telling the story of my life right now. I have stopped a while to see the show.

ONE

I'LL TAKE THE SOUTH

JIMMIE LUNCEFORD AND HIS ORCHESTRA, VOC. SY OLIVER, NEW YORK, 1935

You take the east
Take the west
Take the north
I'll take the South!

IN MY EARLY FORTIES I did what many dream of doing when surprised by the onset of middle age: I dropped everything, packed up and ran away to the south of France.

This embrace was presaged by decades of flirtation. Even in my early teens I had nursed a passion for things Gallic. French Romantic composer Hector Berlioz and chanteuse Edith Piaf loomed largest in my personal pantheon of idols. I made the first of many visits to Paris as a nineteen year old in February 1976, walking around a wintry Right Bank while screwing up enough courage to sidle into the café down the nearest *rue* to enquire whether anyone spoke English. Since no Frenchman in his right mind would confess to this in front of others in a crowded bar, I had been forced to repeat the ritual until exasperation and the bitter cold drove me back to my hotel, where I could finally swot up on the phrases essential to sustaining life. These studies often took place in the corridor outside my room, as my hands were so frozen by exposure on my bleak *touristique* rambles that I cut a suspicious figure, fruitlessly manipulating my key in the door lock with jelly fingers. I was reported to reception twice by a passing chambermaid.

Earlier in the same trip, as I was being swept along Buckingham Palace Road in London by the evening peak-hour tide of people, my head lowered to ensure that my feet landed in unoccupied patches of pavement, I bumped into an oncoming chest.

'I beg your pard . . . *Booker?*'

'Well, well. *Hello to you.*'

'This is amazing,' I remarked with some justification. It *was* a coincidence to bump into an acquaintance from the opposite end of the world on a dark winter's evening in one of London's busiest streets. 'I had no idea you were even in London. What are you doing here?'

'Just on my way back to the place where I'm staying. You've caught me returning from a situation,' he added conspiratorially. 'It's been *steamy.*'

I interpreted this correctly to mean a conquest. We decided to celebrate Booker's good fortune with a beer. It would be my first opportunity to talk at length with someone who, although only a handful of years older than myself, was already practised enough in the ways of the world (through which he'd travelled widely) to have contrived steamy situations in big foreign cities. Travel *and* sex – I had almost no experience of either, and was therefore doubly impressed.

We had first met a few months before in Sydney, when I was a music programmer for a classical radio station, spending my days hunched over a turntable (this was the ancient age of vinyl) listening to Beethoven symphonies. British-born Booker had just been appointed to the announcing staff on the strength of his rich baritone voice, produced from a disproportionately slender frame. It was his task to tell the listener which orchestra would be playing the Fifth Symphony, or Rossini's *William Tell* Overture, after having gathered the information from both the back of the album cover and a brief chat with me when I delivered the records to the radio studio in a sturdy metal trolley. Our haiku-length consultations would take place while a book reading or parliamentary session murmured softly from the large RCA box speaker in a corner of the soundproofed room.

'You see, this isn't exactly my *schtick*,' he explained.

'What – Beethoven, you mean?'

'No, Beethoven's great. With Beethoven – hey! It's all happening.' He was cueing an LP on the turntable, sliding the groove backwards and forwards under the stylus much as trance DJs would do in nightclubs twenty years later, turning the opening of Beethoven's Fifth into a palindrome: *da-da-da-DAW . . . WAD-ad-ad-ad*. 'I mean this,' he clarified, pointing to the vinyl itself. 'I prefer the older stuff. Shellac 78s. I've been collecting them for a few years, casing second-hand shops. People with old records die and their kids think the stuff is worthless. They either throw it away or cart it off to the nearest antique shop. Sometimes you can pick up the most incredible bargains, especially if you're prepared to attack the situation strategically to get the price down. The other day I picked up some Jimmie Luncefords for less than a dollar. Mid-30s recordings, when Sy Oliver was doing the arrangements, including a mint condition copy of *I'll Take The South*. It's good, but the band doesn't sound quite as hot as it did the year before. Now *that* was a classic time. Wait there, I'll just get this symphony under way.'

The red ON AIR light came on as several thousand listeners were suddenly granted access to our room. Booker became sepulchral in tone to prepare them for Beethoven's Fifth, while I maintained a respectful silence and pondered his enthusiasm for music that people only wanted to throw away. The guy's eccentric, I deduced, satisfied that the initial suspicions I entertained upon seeing a twenty-six year old in a cravat had been amply confirmed. Of course, my teenage lack of irony did not regard my *own* capacity to discourse on the relative merits of various recordings of Beethoven's Fifth as being unusual in any way.

There had been a lot to take in from his brief monologue of a moment before, delivered with intellect and discernment. Why did I think of this as being eccentric? Perhaps it was the cultural climate in which I grew up; it was very Anglo-Australian to regard with suspicion those who seemed over-particular. Fussy, it was called. Being fussy with food, for instance, meant that one was difficult to please and, by implication, ungrateful.

I wasn't too discerning when it came to food or clothes, but I *had* become fussy about my music. Two years of floating in a sea of symphonies and sonatas in the vast resources of a radio station's record library had provided me with a head start in knowing about Beethoven and whether or not he was being well played. This might have made me sound snobbish – even arrogant – when passing judgement on performances I had heard, but it was the only reassurance available at the time to the insecure part of me that mistook arrogance for certitude, and certitude for superiority.

And yet this same particularity could become a blinker, I began to realise, as Booker talked about a form of music that I had not taken seriously up to that moment; music you couldn't even hear in stereo, assuming that you could hear it at all under the crackle of a superannuated record surface. If *my* stuff's better than anyone else's, I wondered with the dawning self-doubt of the average teenage tosser, then by what right is he so keen on his? For there was something other than the easy enthusiasm in his manner: there was *gratitude* – passion being too emotive a word for someone who behaved with reserve, spoke with precision and wore a cravat.

Such gratitude for anything considered arcane – a crackly 1935 record of Jimmie Lunceford's band, or even a teenager's new record of Beethoven's Fifth – is called eccentric by those whose taste is usually prescribed by someone else. So these few strange, discordant people are marginalised, along with their taste. This often matters not a whit to the outsiders themselves, even were they to notice. *That* is what makes them eccentric: their blissful, almost unknowing individuality.

Back in that radio studio, I made a mental note that eccentricity was interesting, and that I should seek out others with a similar mindset. Years later it occurred to me that had I been much older than eighteen I might also have been regarded as eccentric. Strategic or assumed non-conformity is considered a brave stance, the prerogative of the young; whereas the sweetness of natural non-conformity – eccentricity – is a quality granted only to those we regard as 'mature'. Worse, it is thought of as a gentle misfortune of age, even middle age, a precursor of senility. This is too long to wait for such a beneficial state of mind. The young should strive for it as soon as they can. Eccentricity is wasted on the old.

'Welcome to the Stack of Shellac. *Your senses will never be the same.*'

Now that I had been made privy to Booker's London adventures, it was a natural progression to be introduced to the objects of his constant interest once we were back in Australia. They shared the vintage of his pleasant 1920s Lower North Shore flat on the top floor of a block that craned over adjacent houses for a generous glimpse of Sydney Harbour. The records were in a room on the harbour side, benefiting from the same privileges that some Australian sports clubs extend to their car parks: the best views.

We approached this aerial Aladdin's cave through a large antechamber housing the instruments and tools that made the music happen: a turntable, a disc cleaning machine that resembled a turntable with a suction nozzle at the end of the tone arm where the stylus should be, record brushes with fine, soft bristles, a small plastic doughnut-shaped spindle mount to help 'centre' some of the more unsteady specimens before playing, a device to gauge the correct 78 rpm playing speed, books that contained lists of record catalogue numbers and session details, and original sheet music from the Depression and before.

One of the song sheets brandished the enigmatic smile of the young Duke Ellington on its cover. On another, a portly Bessie Smith, while a third featured a Louise Brooks look-alike smouldering at an unresponsive young man in a top hat. Despite the harbour breeze wafting through a sliver of open window, a slight mustiness, the smell of old things, hung in the air. An afterthought of two armchairs gave Booker licence to call this his living room.

But these were merely attendant courtiers to the crown jewels that lay beyond: a room lined floor to ceiling with rows of frayed sleeve edges crammed together on metal shelves. Spores had broken away and were growing stalagmite columns of jazz from the off-white shag carpet, clear evidence that Booker's ceaseless hunt for more storage was losing in the race to keep up with his expanding collection. Here was a *bouillon* of echoes; music recorded so long ago lying latent in those countless grooves along with the traces of those who had loved and handled them. They stood ready to play, as potent as they had always been. It felt like a depot of loaded guns.

'How about something wacky?' Booker suggested. 'A vignette for trumpet and vocal obbligato. German, probably late 1920s.'

Even without any identifying sleeve spines or cardboard tabs, he quickly found the record in question and slipped it free of its paper negligée, cradling the rim against his thumb and the spindle hole on his middle finger. Slowly, he tilted it in a circular motion, the overhead light reflecting on its surface allowing him to inspect the condition of the grooves. He then lifted it to eye level, squinting through his glasses to check it was perfectly flat; that the stylus would not be in for a bumpy ride. Cleared for touchdown, the disc was placed on the turntable platter with the care of a child being tucked into bed, and the tone arm levered onto the outer groove, throwing out a warm fizz of surface noise.

A quavering solo trumpet intoned a lament too melodramatic to be sincere. Laughter – a woman's – began to percolate from elsewhere, eventually infecting the trumpeter, who spattered through his instrument before joining the woman in a bizarre wordless duet of mounting hilarity. The merrymakers hooted themselves to a pitch sounding rather like an orgasm, after which they subsided, breathless and exhausted.

The stylus slid diplomatically to the inner groove.

'Well,' I said.

'That's a French pressing, and therefore called *Éclat de rire*,' Booker explained, savouring my speechlessness. 'Obviously a very special moment in that Berlin studio. Now you can say that *you were there*.'

'The title says it all. Did you say post-Weimar Republic vintage? I wouldn't have thought there was much to laugh about. You needed a wheelbarrow of money to buy a beer.'

'Probably why they made it. Now that you're warmed up, let's get to some classic tracks. Do you remember that Jimmie Lunceford I told you about months ago? I've given it a clean and it sounds hotter than I remembered.'

And it did.

This wasn't the tinny, distant sound of His Master's Voice through a horn that had so captivated Nipper the dog. I could hear the slap of a double bass, the sharp articulation of the reeds, the sibilants in Sy Oliver's vocal on the words 'Mason Dixon line'. Nothing sounds as modern as a good sibilant. Enrico Caruso (1873–1921) might have been to the 78 what Elvis Presley became to the LP fifty years later – the artist who drove the technology into the average household – but the great tenor's voice was always a 'woith' on disc because up until the 1920s making an acoustic recording was akin to giving directions to a deaf man through an ear trumpet.

The advent of the microphone and what was at first reluctantly called 'electric' recording changed all that. While the frequency range of 1935's *I'll Take The South* from Jimmie Lunceford's Orchestra wouldn't have stretched Nipper's hearing, being only slightly beyond the capability of a good telephone line, and the surface noise from the grooves covered everything with that thin sizzle, one could hear all the band's working parts, the *inside* of the music.

The insouciance of the syncopation couldn't fool me. This was *hot*.

'You're right,' I said to Booker over the music. '*I am there*. And here I was thinking that 78 records were just a run-up to the time when they could finally do it properly.'

'It was a long run-up, in that case,' he replied. 'One of the first records I ever bought of *anything* as a kid was a Cliff Richard. That was the late 50s and – guess what? – it was a 78. We're talking about a history of fifty years as the predominant reproduction format, and less than twenty-five years before CDs and digital sound hit the market. Not much of a gap between shellac and the little silver discs. And for much of those fifty years they had electric recording, even if there were only a couple of mikes to play with. You listen; those engineers knew exactly what they were doing, and they figured it out early. For me, the first five or ten years after the microphone hit the scene – late 20s, early 30s – *that's* when it all came together in a technical sense. If you like the sort of stuff that I do, the timing of that advance was fortuitous, because all the great musos were around and on form.'

'They sound it. I suppose when they were cutting a side in those days the band just ploughed on regardless.'

'That's right. Unless there was some irretrievable collapse in the playing you made sure that the three minutes of whatever you were doing went down onto the wax original. There was more risk in making a record than now. None of this endless multi-track crap; the only way to fix a glitch by the pianist was to have everyone do the whole thing again. *Listen* to these guys; this playing is *dangerous*. They're doing it for real.'

Jimmie and the band had finished their close harmony vocal repeat of Sy's solo and were swinging to a big finish. A final flick of saxophones and trombones, and it was over. Booker carefully lifted the tone arm from the disc.

'So this is your stuff?' I pointed at the record he was returning to its sleeve.

'My *schtick*? Yes. I call it jazztrash. That doesn't mean that it's rubbish. It just happens to be music that not a lot of people want, judging by how much of it turns up in second-hand shops. I prefer early swing, not so much the later stuff that was conflated by the white big bands of Dorsey and Miller into 1940s popular music, although that's good too, but the small black bands that were sprouting up everywhere and heading for New York and Chicago during the Wall Street crash days and the Depression. Nobody swings like these black guys. I like stride piano too, with the bouncing left hand. Art Tatum has amazing frills, but Fats Waller is hard to beat.' Booker indicated the upright piano against the wall. 'I do some playing myself. And in art, as in life, I like stuff that is "out there". Eastern European gypsy music from the 20s; classic theremin . . .'

'Theremin?'

'The world's first electronic instrument, invented by a Russian just after the end of the First World War. You play it without actually touching anything. Very handy when you're wanting spooky music for 1950s science-fiction movies. You should hear my copy of one playing *Lover Come Back To Me* in 1931.'

'If you say so.'

'I also have a talk, purportedly by Count Leo Tolstoy, recorded in 1909, and English library music from the 40s and 50s. Then there's the quality material: stacks of Ellington, including many of the mid-30s recordings that even Ellington fans tend to underrate, a lot of Benny Goodman, early Dorsey brothers . . .'

'Slow down! We might have to take them one at a time. That's a big room in there. But try some out on me. They're the sort of change I need after a working week of Mozart.'

'Sure. I think this calls for a kir. Ever had one? The French version of Ribena. Just mix a little with some white wine . . . or champagne, if you have more spare cash than I do. *Your senses will never be the same.* And as for another hit from the Stack of Shellac . . . hey! Since you were there . . . *Éclat de rire* with those wacky Germans. Let's do that one again.'

The woman and the trumpeter laughed. This time I joined them.

Twenty years later, when it occurred to me that I didn't laugh as much any more, I received a bombshell communiqué from Booker in Paris.

He had left broadcasting and Australia for the City of Light to attempt a new career as a cultural attaché at an embassy. Perhaps he imagined, as did I, that the seductive mix of white linen suits at diplomatic parties, his '*hello to you*' opener – by now fine-tuned to staggering effect – and the impeccable French he had spoken since childhood would be his passport out of a bureaucracy he had endured for years into something more interesting. Instead, his new world turned out to be just another bureaucracy. It all came adrift after two years with a contretemps about timesheets and managerial practice. Booker left, clutching his dignity and sheafs of letterhead.

Once the embassy door had closed behind him, sealing off the prospect of a glorious future in international relations, he had a discomfiting realisation. By now in his mid-forties, he was unemployable in the mercilessly downsizing 90s. Left to his own devices, he mooched around Paris for months, playing some piano gigs and becoming a frequent hunter for shellac at the *marchés aux puces*, the flea markets near the *portes* on the city perimeter.

And now came Booker's letter, the first I had received from him for some time. A new friend from the flea-market circuit had offered him a place to stay down in the Gard as an alternative to the tumult and expense of Paris, and he had accepted. It was goodbye city blues, *hello to you* small town retreat. He was taking the South.

Jimmie Lunceford never knew much about downsizing, or being unemployable. He never knew much about being in his mid-forties, either. In July 1947 – he had just turned forty-five – Lunceford was signing autographs during a personal appearance in a music store in Seaside, Oregon, when he dropped dead. A heart attack was deemed the official verdict, although gossips hinted at poisoning by a racist restaurant owner. Either way, Lunceford's early demise was in keeping with an emerging jazz tradition. Drugs, the bottle, exhaustion or plain misadventure – these guys and gals dropped like flies. Clearly, the ability to swing came at some cost. Jimmie should have been more careful when he recorded a song in 1934 called *Rhythm Is Our Business.*

One morning I realised that I was close to Jimmie Lunceford's fatal age, causing me to entertain a strange logic. If all the good swingers like Lunceford and Gershwin – or Mozart, for that matter – tended to die early, and I was still alive, it followed that I was unable to swing. This was a big revelation. For me, swinging was not just a matter of syncopating on a saxophone, bending the rhythm so that the underlying pulse could jump out and give your system a lift; rather, swinging was syncopating *life*, bending the stolid four-in-the-bar rhythm that is given to us, coming up with a freewheeling new improvisation on that old tune. And if I had to describe it like this, then I obviously couldn't do it.

My Anglo-Saxon genes were largely to blame ('*nobody* swings like these black guys') but the major cause was a matter of training – or lack of it. The long-planned swing induction course had not eventuated. My visits to Booker and his collection were all too infrequent, and suddenly he packed the shellac and moved it to the northern hemisphere in an industrial-scale evacuation. Ten thousand records now lived happily with their owner in a light-filled rustic house in the dream world of the south of France.

Meanwhile, Side A of my working life had played without interruption for twenty-five years. The record was about to flip over to a Side B that might sound like more of the same and play for just as long. It was time to pause a little on the inner groove.

At this point I heard another recording of *I'll Take The South* from 1935, by the Mississippi-born singer Cleopatra Brown, which features a more complete lyric than the largely instrumental Lunceford version:

Every little swallow in the tree
Has packed their nest and gone
You can bet your life
I'm gonna follow that swallow from now on!
You take the Alps
Take Paree
As for me
I'll take the South!

Cleo possessed a tiny voice, but this was a loud siren song, one with navigational tips. I wrote to Booker in what I imagined to be classic swing-speak – language of the cool – announcing that I intended to follow the swallow. Were any other rooms going for rent in his old town? He replied with a warning: the place was so indifferent to tourism that there were no hotels, but his landlord might be able to find something. How long was I planning to stay?

Two months, I thought. That was the amount of time Artie Shaw spent in Mexico when he walked away from his career in 1939. Two months, then he came back with *Frenesi*. It was sufficient time in which to find myself a new song.

I found an atlas, opened it at the map of France, traced my finger south of Paris and west of the Alps towards the Gard, and began to imagine the fine detail of my midlife escape.

TWO

AVANT DE MOURIR

SVEND ASMUSSEN, KØBENHAVN, 1940

T WO-AND-A-HALF HOURS out of Paris, the fast train banked slowly to the right, away from the *luxe* of Provence and into a part of France in which I was assured the French still live.

It was late March. The countryside through the window was colouring from grey to an incipient green as we rocketed closer to the Mediterranean. In Paris a brisk stroll in the cool air made the skin of my face crustier than the outside of a baguette, and the trees at the tip of the Île St Louis were still brazenly nude. Here in the more conservative South nature was covering up as quickly as possible. And yet the new spring layers of blossom and early leaf growth failed to disguise the harshness and angularity of the landscape beneath; florid lingerie on a lean body.

Booker's letter sounded promising. 'It's a deal,' he concluded. 'I've spoken to Crumb and he has offered you his basement at a mate's rate. You'll find it to be quite salubrious by underfloor standards, featuring a view of passing swans. I would have offered you space in the shack that he lets out to me, but it's just a renovated goat shed with room for only one old goat at a time. Yours, B.'

This begged the question of where his massive record collection had ended up. Space in the backwoods of the Gard must be at a premium if Booker could find only a former livestock habitat for himself, and a hole in the ground for me with nothing to see but swans' feet. On the plus side, the rent Booker had negotiated was cheap enough for me to last out the two months in a place in which guest accommodation was rare. His landlord – soon to be mine – was the mysterious friend from the Parisian flea markets at whose invitation Booker had headed south. He, too, was a record collector with a pile of 78s somewhere in the house above my ceiling. I presumed that on balmy spring evenings, when he wanted to share his shellac with some new company, my landlord could wrench open a hatch in the floor and let me out for a breath of music and a glimpse of swan above the waterline.

The TGV slowed and slid into the station at Avignon. Ah, Avignon! City of the popes, locale for some of the charming Alphonse Daudet stories written in the calm of his windmill! I cupped my ear in search of the sound of a distant tambour beating out the farandole for all those happy couples dancing on the famous bridge. The gesture encouraged a guy standing nearby to repeat himself. I thought he'd been asking the time. His susurration was actually a sales pitch.

'You want some *sheet*?'

I glanced around the reception hall. Several other peddlers of low-grade hashish were making similar approaches to idlers. Now that most of the trainload of travellers had spilled through into the late afternoon, leaving behind a handful of people, the station looked decidedly seedy. Daudet would have been safer in his windmill.

My sense of creeping unease was dispelled by a hasty hand-shake. 'Quickly,' said Booker. 'The Kangoo's just outside and the engine's running. If we're not back there in a minute it'll be either booked or stolen. Both, if the Avignon parking police are on form.'

We expressed our regrets to the gathering horde of Moroccans in bulging herbal jackets and hurried out to the car park. A large van emitting a loud diesel purr was attracting the attention of some youths with fuzzy top lips. None of them appeared to be a parking policeman. They moved on to the next vehicle as Booker swung open the rear doors for my suitcase.

'Plenty of room in there,' I observed.

'I'm a gigging muso these days. There has to be enough room for a double bass.'

The van's doors closed out the din of car horns and clatter of suitcase wheels, and another sound world took their place. A 1930s orchestra snaked out from under the dashboard with

Cole Porter's *Night And Day*. The throb of the accompaniment led into the song's opening line from Fred Astaire:

> *Like the beat-beat-beat of the tom-toms*
> *When the jungle shadows fall*

Shadows fell across the rain-streaked ramparts of Avignon as we trundled west. The fourteenth-century popes here would have known these same ramparts, I reflected. They were supposed to be jolly days, when the city was the official centre of Christianity.

This grey spring day was not one of them. Peak-hour traffic ignored the prompts of flashing lights, and litter patrolled the unkempt footpaths on a persistent wind, a poor relation of the notorious mistral. Winter here was an uncooperative tenant, refusing to quit the premises before the decorators were due to arrive. The place looked as exhausted as I felt. It had been a non-stop trip from Sydney. Now that we were on a bridge crossing the Rhône, I looked down at the sluggish flow of the river. Nobody was dancing a farandole on the old *pont*.

Fred wound up his vocal. For all the trademark nonchalance of his singing, *Night And Day*'s lyric is more about obsession than devotion; even the melody keeps sticking on the fifth note – called the dominant, strangely – of the scale. Porter didn't intend all of his love songs to be comforters.

'A sinister version,' I remarked. (Critiques should always be shorter than your average haiku.) It was typical that our first conversation after a long absence should begin with a comment on music, rather than an exchange of personal news.

'A classic,' Booker countered – the highest praise, 'and no mere *version*. That's the original, recorded in New York City, November 1932, when Porter's musical *The Gay Divorce* was playing on Broadway. Fred was still a stage star. He hadn't yet cracked it in Hollywood.'

'So he's not singing to Ginger there?'

'No – Claire Luce. Ginger had to wait until they made the film of the musical two years later. By then the title had changed to *The Gay Divorcée*. I don't think the adjective had today's meaning back in 1934, but clearly someone didn't want any confusion surrounding Fred.'

'I don't see how *anyone* could be confused with Ginger around. What's that last line? He wants to spend his life making love to her, day and night.'

'And night and day.'

'Gene Kelly might have gone for it at a pinch, but Fred Astaire? I find it harder to imagine.'

'Fred is underestimated as a singer, in my opinion. I've been restoring some of his early recordings, including tracks he recorded in the 20s with George Gershwin. He is always in tune, his phrasing is so natural that he makes you think it's effortless, and the words are clear. Returning to the Ginger issue, don't forget that as a dancer, he would have been fit – even in old age. Didn't he end up married to a jockey?'

Consideration of this was elbowed aside by Fred's next vocal as the van headed into the *département* of the Gard and the evening's destination of Uzès. A former duchy perched on a hill, its old palace towers and cathedral spires crown a city whose centre is a chic model of preservation from the past, with a burgeoning population of British and northern European retirees. The transformation of what must have been an attractively dirty city fifty years ago into the attractively clean one of today seems not to bother the few remaining French who can still afford to live there, but it infuriates some of the longer-term immigrants who complain, without a trace of irony, that the experience of living in the South has been made inauthentic by the influx of foreigners. An Englishman, packing up his house to move closer to the Pont du Gard, told me phlegmatically that Uzès had turned into 'a medieval Disneyland for Germans'.

One of the earlier waves of foreign arrivals included Booker's parents. Their house was on the edge of Uzès, bordering a field of what would become sunflowers later in the spring. Power lines leading to an electrical substation directly across the street transected the view of distant hills from their front balcony. Next to this was the local lunatic asylum, a building that seemed disproportionately large for a city the size of Uzès. Some of the residents would wave to us from upper-storey windows while we drank our end-of-day apéritifs. Being higher than the power lines, the view from their rooms must have been spectacular.

Approaching the house was difficult because of the skill required to turn off the road and pass through the front gate. The narrow street was a rifle barrel for the local drivers who drove faster than a speeding bullet and the angle of the drive was extremely acute. Too fast, and one could overshoot; too slow, and there was every possibility of hitting an oncoming vehicle. Such precision was akin to re-entering the earth's atmosphere from orbit, yet Booker was able to swing in the wide body of his van without a hitch. We left Fred Astaire under the dashboard and stepped out into the back garden alongside a line of washing drying rapidly in the wind. Perhaps not all previous re-entries had been as successful, for I noticed a dent in the passenger door on the driver's side.

'Pig,' he explained.

Booker's octogenarian mother raised her evening scotch in greeting as we walked in. Whether or not the Swiss finishing school she attended in the early 1930s was the source of Norma's unaffected gentility, I couldn't say, but with the advancing years she had been clever – or lucky – enough to merge this quality with a disarming pragmatism. 'You will come back and see us again soon, won't you?' she had asked me with graceful inflections at the end of our previous meeting. 'Otherwise I shall be dead.'

Instead, she was healthily alive, and it was I who trudged up to the guest bedroom for an appointment with a coma after waving back lethargically at the neighbours.

Morning brought with it the sound of a distant violin, reassuring me as I woke that the first stage of my escape to rustic pleasure had been completed.

Getting to France had been easy; finding the way to the source of the violin could be more difficult. The Booker family *maison* had been reconfigured to suit the age and convenience of its owners, with challenging results. The main stairway could only be accessed through Norma's bedroom, previously the garage. In view of this impracticality, a new wing had been built to accommodate a circular stairway that had to be approached via the laundry. Guests who were unfamiliar with the layout had no way of finding their way from one floor to another. The problem was compounded by Norma's habit of assiduously locking all windows and exterior doors every evening in order to keep the cats in and the gypsies out. Her poor hearing meant that calls for help from upstairs fell on deaf ears. One visitor had been trapped for the greater part of a day, vainly signalling his distress with a white handkerchief to the cheerily waving residents in the building across the road.

But on this sunny spring French morning, the beginning of a new chapter in my life, all doors were open. I boldly stepped through a curtain of underpants and spiralled my way down to the music.

'Hello to you, and welcome to the thrilling tones of Svend Asmussen in the classic tune *Avant de mourir*.'

My host was still in his dressing gown, seated before a large computer screen on which various graphs were unfurling. And there, on either of the long side walls, was the famous collection, not sharing some antique shed with the ghost of a goat after all, but ranged here floor to ceiling on custom-made, very thick, and very – *very* – lime green shelves. (Mental note for later: ask about colour choice *and* pig.) The records that had looked like dishevelled itinerants in Booker's Sydney flat appeared more at home here, stacked evenly in their brightly coloured compartments, and dressed to kill in crisp, new cardboard sleeves. Subtle down lighting where the built-ins met the roof suffused the textured display of thousands of edges with a pleasant glow. An array of equipment snuggled up the wall to Booker's left, its inscrutable front panels demonstrating how much the technology of playing with sound had developed since my first hearing of Jimmie Lunceford.

Two large microphones stood atop a rickety plastic table halfway down the room. They were mounted on sprung cradles to cancel out vibration, and protected from the popping gusts of over-emphatic talkers by homemade wind shields. These consisted of wire coat hangers bent into circular frames, each supporting a stretched membrane of pale brown fabric. I looked closer. They were the gussets from women's pantyhose.

'An effective solution requiring extensive field research,' said Booker with mock self-congratulation. 'You'll find that no one ever pops through a gusset.'

Resting on slender legs, the silhouettes of two loudspeakers faced us from the end of the room, framed by two glass doors that led to a high hedge and the emerging stalks of the flower field next door. They were in the optimal position for listening from Booker's seat at the computer, but not for entertaining. One of them was toppled by my gyrating bottom at a later impromptu dance gathering, fracturing an original pressing of *Holiday For Strings*.

Cables of varying thicknesses curled everywhere, even in conduits under the floor; clusters of records had been assembled for special purposes and leaned against the skirting board; headphones, digital tape players, discarded sleeves, dog-eared old magazines and sheets of notepaper with pencilled scrawls were strewn across a benchtop. On the rare patch of available wall a photo of uncertain vintage featured a female singer wearing shorts and a Betty Boop expression, encircled by the ogling boys in the band. Some of them were pointing their trombones at her.

Here among sunflowers and wine co-operatives in the south of France, Booker had created a simple but functional sound studio.

'This is good,' I said, using all the technical jargon at my disposal. 'We could do stuff here.'

'I'm already doing it,' Booker declared, clicking the mouse on its Pamela Anderson pad to stop the violinist mid-phrase. 'Haven't you noticed something about Svend Asmussen?'

'Apart from the fact that he's ripped off The Platters' version of *My Prayer*?'

This observation seemed to please him. 'Not at all. Svend was first.'

'Svend plays a mean violin.'

'That he does. I often feel he outdoes Stéphane Grappelli in the style department. He's Danish. The recording dates from 1940.'

'1940? It sounds great for its age.'

'*Voilà*. You *have* noticed. It has received the Treatment.'

The Treatment was Booker's new profession. His days as a broadcaster and diplomatic ornament behind him, he had become a cleaner. But this was a different sort of cleaning. Using his shelves of gadgets and a discerning ear, he could take a technical dustpan and brush to the sounds his old records made, smoothing over the bumps, vacuuming away the crackle and hiss, bringing back some of the clarity blunted over the years by other people's styli. Booker could change the sound by literally redrawing the graphs on the screen of his computer, picking out the scratches and tracing over the holes left behind with a deft stroke of his mouse-turned-electronic pen. He was careful not to introduce elements into the recordings that had not been there in the first place. As he had told me earlier, the engineers of those days knew what they were doing.

Fred Astaire was fresh again, Duke Ellington's band swung just like the old days, and Svend Asmussen – while not about to fool me into thinking he had recorded *Avant de mourir* yesterday – could at least be enjoyed without the listener having to condescend to the recording's age. Booker's collection, for so long a hobby, was turning into a source of income, something he could share with other people on a commercial scale. Transferred from bulky shellac onto shiny compact discs, the music could travel to a new audience, one that would pay collectors and boutique sound restorers like Booker for the ease of access.

My attention was drawn to something that looked like a cigar box, bearing the vivid design of a fanged woman with a lascivious stare, sturdy torso and thick-ankled legs. The title *Devil Girl* blazed from its lid in large comic book-cover lettering, creating an effect both funny and slightly unsettling.

'Now *that's* a collector's item,' I commented. 'Who did it?'

'Your landlord. I'm not sure if Crumb is in town at the moment, but it's high time you were installed in your subterranean redoubt. We'll leave after lunch. In the meantime, I'll shower. Then we can spin a few sides.'

The van wound further west through Languedoc villages with windows shuttered against the chill of the afternoon as people took their stomachs to bed. Plane trees still lined stretches of straight road, though their numbers were diminishing year by year. In 1900, there had been nearly three million *arbres d'alignement*; now there were less than 400,000. Recent statistics revealed that the French, while experiencing half the rate of heart attacks of the English, were twice as likely to be killed in road accidents. The romantically named incident of *embrasser des platanes* was a common cause of fatalities, about 750 a year, including the writer Albert Camus, whose car hugged a tree in 1950.

In a leap of deduction worthy of Inspector Clouseau, the government decided to blame it all on the trees. Since it was impossible to prevent wine-soaked partygoers from swerving off the road, the State would clear from their errant trajectories anything too slow to jump out of the way. Trees refusing to move would be taken away by force. Houses and pensioners were exempted from the swathes cut by official buzz-saws, and pigs would be taken care of in the hunting season.

Not all pigs, as Booker's dented Kangoo proved, although in his case there was no question of being wine-soaked, or even veering towards a tree. The way he told it, the pig had run into *him*.

'I was returning from an afternoon party in a surprisingly coherent state. The sun was still up and visibility was good. There was quite a bit of traffic. All of a sudden, a *sanglier* charged out from some brush along the side of the road and slammed into the side of me. It was November, so the unfortunate animal was probably dodging bullets coming from everywhere; those idiots usually take out a few cyclists during the season as well. Anyway, it gave me one hell of a jolt. I drove those last few kilometres to the village *very* carefully and needed a couple of *rouges* at the Commerce to get over it. Most of the regulars there look as if they've taken out a few pigs in their time, so I explained to them why I looked shaky.'

'What did they say?'

'They wanted to know why I hadn't stopped to pick up the pig. *Sanglier* may not be our idea of heaven, but for some it is manna when one offers itself to passing motorists. I could hear everybody salivating.'

The sound of *Avant de mourir* floated back into my mind – violin sliding stylishly above shimmering vibes in an easy tango – as I began to think about the sort of place where the locals drool over roadkill. Why was I going there, and what did I think I was going to do in a basement for two months? All of the answers to the first question I had entertained thus far sounded either self-indulgent or banal, and as for the second . . . well, it would answer itself in time. *Live*, I supposed, as if the experience of living would be richer in old stone; something medieval with a garnish of Nature on the side. What a great setting for a life! Within days I might be slapping the back of a friendly local in a bar, eagerly preparing my next dinner, entertaining deep thoughts among the ruins of some Romanesque monastery on an isolated hilltop, or conjugating verbs with Juliette Binoche.

The Cévennes, hitherto a quaint ornament on the horizon, now began to rear up ahead of us in a dramatic panorama.

More than a hundred years earlier, Robert Louis Stevenson had wandered through them with his donkey. He knew all about adventure, and here was obviously the place for it. My first question was answered. I presupposed this to be a place where life was more exciting, or better still, more fun. And with all that good music waiting to be heard in a goat shed, my blues would be banished in a blaze of swing.

Perhaps the answers to such questions are *always* disconcertingly short and banal, just like those in self-help books. Did the gregarious and untroubled people I was bound to meet here even bother asking them in the first place? Probably not – they were too busy slapping each other's backs. Voltaire had pronounced on the uselessness of metaphysical speculation back in the eighteenth century, and the people around here had taken him seriously.

I hoped that my experiences over the next few months would bring me around to his point of view, because the habit of agonising about life had become impossible to break and exhausting to maintain. Displacement was essential. The list of those I had left behind included *me*, and I did not want to discover when unpacking in the basement that I had inadvertently brought myself along for the ride. My addiction to thinking was to be left behind at home. Yet while one can hide the vodka bottle from the recovering alcoholic, a person's brain has the nasty tendency to seek out its owner. My tactic of trying to put it off the trail with the distraction of adventure was undoubtedly simplistic, but it would also be pleasurable; the sort of therapeutic pleasure that has to be sought – *avant de mourir.*

'Booker, do you have that Svend Asmussen track with you?'

'Of course.'

'Play it again. It makes me feel . . . *justified*.'

Forty kilometres southwest of Uzès we drove out of the loose weave of country roads and onto the major thoroughfare linking the city of Nîmes further south with St Hippolyte-du-Fort. Turning right, we began heading in the direction of the latter, a curtain of escarpment to our left drawing the mountains ever closer.

'Goat shed HQ. Brace yourself – *you are here,*' announced Booker in the plumped-up, urgent tones of a 1940s newsreel commentator.

It was as if he had waved a wand. A grey stone stage set materialised from nowhere, tucked up the steep slope of the escarpment, ending just below the topmost ridge. Only an ancient castle had been rash enough to peep above this natural line of protective rock, and it looked to have had its head shot off. Below this, the irregular jumble of spires, turrets, tiled roofs and crooked walls conveyed a wicked animation. Were I to look away for a few seconds the buildings might jump up and instantly rearrange themselves.

Flocks of birds filled the space between rooftops and hilltop like restless quotation marks. Two bridges spanned a river on which bobbed many ducks. In their midst, regal but incongruous, were two white swans, the ones whose feet would decorate my days. How many quaint visual clichés did one place need? Heaped all together like this, however, the effect – from a distance – was quirky, unexpectedly dramatic, beautiful.

We turned off the main road, crossed a large open space that would fill with cars on weekends, and edged carefully onto a bridge over the river. The operation required even more microsurgical precision than the Booker family front gate.

'Tight fit,' I observed helpfully.

'I wouldn't blame our Pont Vieux. It was here before the cars. Since the end of the eleventh century, in fact. That's the Vidourle below us. Apart from the last couple of days it has been a dry year, so the river is behaving itself.'

The van squeezed through to the far side of the old bridge, turned under some large supporting arches and rolled down an incline of gravel to stop alongside the Vidourle. Water was everywhere. The sound of the fine rain drumming softly on the Kangoo's roof humbled everything else into silence. Only an occasional quack penetrated the hush.

Thick walls burst from the ground to our left and soared up at least five levels to form a sort of medieval high-rise. They were not sheer; a couple of floors up we could see the edge of an outdoor terrace bordered by long boxes of flowers just beginning their decorative descent down the stone fascia. Further along, a corner turret with windows sliced up and down its circumference looked as if part of the ruin we had seen earlier had tumbled down from the hilltop and landed upside down in the ground, letting its castellations take root.

Next to us, directly underneath the flower-bordered terrace, stood a brown double-door.

'This,' said Booker, 'is your basement.'

My visions of swans' feet went happily out the window. 'But I thought . . . ?'

'You thought that you would be underground? Ah . . . but you'll note I called it a *basement*, not a *cellar*. It is all relative. You will discover that you do indeed live under Crumb's ground floor, but since the riverbank is much lower still, you are – at least from the point of view of the swans – very much up in the air. Moreover, this is a multistorey basement. Shall we?'

Through the door my impression of an inverted world was

confirmed. This basement had an entrance lobby, from which stairs ascended to a small first-floor sitting room and kitchen overlooking the river. A wooden platform on high stilts served as a mezzanine bedroom, accessible via a precipitous ladder climb that surely could only be attempted when sober. At the top of the stairs a tunnel carved out of the rock led upward again to two hollows housing a small shower recess and toilet, placing the tenant's evacuations, most appropriately, in the very bowels of the earth. If you slipped in the shower it was possible to slide back down the tunnel and onto the main stairs, ending up at the front door. Alice, the White Rabbit and the hole came to my mind. This was not so much basement living as cave dwelling. I would be the town troglodyte.

'I'll take it,' I said.

'Good. We can finalise terms with Crumb when he gets back. I'll be away for a few days at the big annual antique record fair in the Wimbledon Dog Stadium. There's always a lot on sale, but one has to arrive early, identify the prey, and stalk it through the morning. It's my biggest annual Shellac Safari and it pays to be ready and equipped. I'm going in the van.'

Booker drove off – Great White Shellac Hunter – with the strains of *Avant de mourir* from the Kangoo's open window evaporating above the soft splash of the river, leaving me alone in my new cave to unpack. Life begins now, I noted while going up the tunnel to the bathroom. Returning some minutes later, I noted it again. Now that I was 'living', what *was* I going to do?

THREE

THE FOLKS WHO LIVE ON THE HILL

MAXINE SULLIVAN, ACC. CLAUDE THORNHILL AND
HIS ORCHESTRA, NEW YORK, 1937

Our verandah will command a view of meadows green
The sort of view that seems to want to be seen

WHAT A POPULAR PLACE the south of France is!
Millions flock there to get away from it all, only to
discover that all of *it* has flocked there as well. Some of the
multitudes are French, but many come from elsewhere, drawn
to this mythic land of pleasure by any number of change-of-
life books. Reading about sunshine and cheap wine as they
huddle under the gloom of northern skies, tired and pale
office workers are inspired to dream of their own sleepy farmhouse waiting in some splendid acreage to be discovered and
renovated.

Of course, there are only so many sleepy farmhouses to
go around, and with such demand, Paradise became too

expensive for most of us a long time ago. Dewy-eyed shoppers clustering around Provençal real estate windows now need profoundly deep pockets. Those of us who are not successful actors or retrenched merchant bankers must therefore look beyond Provence, scavenging ever more remote parts of the countryside for anything that pre-dates the Second World War. And so the ripples of affluence move westwards, with tiny hamlets far from the playgrounds of the Côte d'Azur becoming the newest havens of designer rusticity for young millionaires or recent retirees. Granite-topped kitchen benches, dishwashers and saunas are installed in stone rooms inhabited hundreds of years ago by penniless farm workers with bad teeth, plus their sheep.

Building works on this scale do not happen without the owners experiencing the sort of trauma that makes us chuckle when we read about it in their book. As they agonise over colour charts, or apply for a second mortgage to cover the central heating installation bill, new arrivals realise that urban anxiety has been replaced by a country version. Yet the ones I met seem a happy lot. Their dream is close at hand (even if the builder frequently isn't) and obstacles are always faced more amenably when there is a vine, a goat or *boulangerie* outside the window.

The former French owners of these properties, for whom rusticity was never as life-enhancing, also harbour a desire for change. Theirs is satisfied more easily by leaving town after receipt of an astonishing sum from the English or Dutch couple who thought the rat-infested barn and damp-addled bathroom possessed such 'character'. Thousands of mod con villas in spanking new suburbs around regional city centres are full of retired *agriculteurs*, or their now-wealthy heirs, rejoicing over their windfalls.

I would only be passing through, as I lacked the means to permanently enrich the offspring of an impoverished farmer, but I still wanted to have a little of what has by now been had by half of Europe. Fortunately, the thrill of adventure for me doesn't come from being original. Instead, I would be proudly unfashionable, which is what going to the south of France has become, since *everybody* has done it. Certain magazines led me to believe that the *fashionistas* were selling up and moving eastwards to Slovenia. If these tales of defection were true, perhaps only ordinary, unfashionable people might be left in this Languedoc village. Then I would feel right at home.

Waking late the next morning – a consequence of either jet lag, or the tomb-like darkness created by the closed shutters below the level of my platform bed – I climbed carefully down the ladder into the living room. Here was my new simplicity: no radio or television to turn on, no familiar books to open. It was very quiet. After savouring this simplicity for thirty seconds I decided to take a walk before beginning my charm offensive at the local café.

Mist hung over the village after the night's rain, coating my face in a fine spray as I stepped out. A tiny bridge crossed a spring welling from the base of a high wall; no mere trickle, but a curtain of water flowing with the force of a river that collected in a small reservoir and spilled over into the Vidourle to continue its seaward journey in the open air.

Narrow streets threaded uphill between rows of high house frontages that were heavily rendered, grey and featureless. At one point I wandered through an arcade with low arches running along one side. Light could only reach down here with effort, for the buildings crowded out the sky by huddling for safety under the looming canopy of the escarpment to the south. You couldn't trust passers-by back in the Middle Ages.

The streets were strangely quiet for ten o'clock in the morning. No hearty peasant types came blustering through their front doors. Pigeons rummaged undisturbed between cobblestones. Blue wall plaques commemorated distinguished former residents. A certain Monsieur Florian

(1755–1794) was described as a *fabuliste*. Pascal Vallongue (1763–1806) merited the more exuberant title *Général du Génie*.

A woman on a bicycle raced out from a side street. Her hair was bright orange with dark roots, and she was wearing a short red sleeveless top and tie-dyed pants. She looked very fit, with the tautness of frame due more to vigorous exercise than a strict diet, and could probably have pedalled her bike all day. There were dark circles under her eyes, something I would come to notice in many French women, whose pallor was such a contrast to the cultivated bronzing of the new-comers, with their improbable glow of health. The people who flew south for a weekend – or a summer – of rest never looked as if they were in need of it, whereas the locals here showed every sign of being completely drained by indolence. That, or light deprivation in these gloomy streets. I wondered how I would scrub up after two months in a basement. Colleagues, never noticing my absence in the first place, might suggest upon my return that I looked as if I needed a holiday.

The Orange Flash turned and whizzed in my direction, appraising me with raccoon eyes before muttering a single word as she passed by. Too late, I realised she had said *bonjour*. The greeting was so surprising that I had no time to process the intention behind the word. Experience would teach me there had been no intention other than casual civility. In small places like this, greeting strangers is expected.

Continuing my trek up a steeper incline in the direction of the high ridge, the sound of my footsteps was muffled as street paving gave way to dirt. And then, for the second time in as many days, I heard a violin, this time real rather than recorded, playing phrases of what sounded like a Scottish dance tune, broken off and repeated. The music came from a balcony just above my head. A sign hanging over the doorway opposite bore the inscription *Peintre* over a pen and ink drawing of the Pont Vieux. Here was an enclave of quiet industry, the pleasing scratch of a fiddle on one side of the path, that of a quill on the other.

Somewhere far off a bell rang the hour, the sound mingling with the snatches of melody overhead, and Maxine Sullivan slid onto the platter of my mental jukebox, singing *The Folks Who Live On The Hill*. The track begins with the chime of a tubular bell before the first 'getaway' line

Someday we'll build a home on a hilltop high
You and I

The lyric was penned by Oscar Hammerstein II, who must have had a thing about hills; he claimed they were alive when he wrote *The Sound of Music* twenty years later. This earlier effort was for the 1937 film *High, Wide and Handsome*, a musical western set in the grand expanses of 1850s Pennsylvania that is a precursor to Hammerstein's later and greater musical western effort with Richard Rodgers – *Oklahoma!* One assumes it is the country that is high, wide and handsome in this collaboration with composer Jerome Kern, and not actor Randolph Scott, who leaves his wife (and former saloon bar tabletop vocalist) Irene Dunne to go off and build oil pipelines not long after she has conjured up an image of their anticipated domestic idyll in the film's most enduring song.

Despite her on-screen singing of *Folks* in a wedding dress, Irene's version is not as persuasive as that by Maxine Sullivan (1911–1987) recorded the same year. No one in their right mind would exchange Maxine's pipes for anything bigger. Even in these first recording sessions of her career she had learned the lesson of Bing Crosby: the microphone is your confessor, not your megaphone. She delivers the song in what is almost an undertone, as if she is dreaming aloud. Many of her notes would not have made it across the footlights of a theatre stage. The slight jazzing of the melody towards the end seems a shy, whispered aside. Hers is a sort of chamber music, operating on a discreet level far removed from the more orchestral blaze of big band swing.

Perhaps this explains why someone – maybe her musical director at the time, pianist Claude Thornhill – looked at this young, soft-toned black jazz singer from Pennsylvania and decided she should record . . . *Loch Lomond*! Success can come from bizarre ideas. This one turned into a hit record, and was soon followed by Sullivan versions of *Annie Laurie*, *Molly Malone* and *Darling Nellie Gray*. Sensing that being cast as a champion of Scottish folk songs might not be helpful in maintaining a jazz career, and having handed over much of her earnings from radio, film (*St Louis Blues*, *Going Places*) and touring to a succession of managers, Maxine took time away from singing in her early forties to study the flugelhorn, valve trombone . . . and nursing. Taking a mid-career break was an unusual thing to do in the 1950s, more so if you were a woman, and black. Perhaps Maxine just had to do *something* while in the zone described delicately in show business as 'between engagements'.

Was I thinking about Maxine for reasons other than the tolling of a bell? Having nothing better to do as of today than stand under a fiddler's balcony in a remote place, it was necessary for me to take a constructive view of my new condition of indolence by making a parallel between her career shift and mine. This was because a strange and uncomfortable feeling had crept over me. There could be no doubt: it was guilt, and its onset was going to ruin my morning.

I had expected some withdrawal symptoms as the Protestant work ethic oozed from my system, but hoped to laze for a few weeks before breaking into a sweat. Instead, I was only two mornings away from a desk, barely halfway up a hill, and already wondering if I should take up the flugelhorn. It would be embarrassing if someone caught me in the act of doing nothing. Get over it! Wasn't I trying to discover whether bohemianism could become my natural state? Instead, I was worried about the prospect of not being worried. Learning to do nothing with unashamed flair was going to be hard work. This was my adventure's first challenge. In order to swing, one first had to be able to hang loose.

What of Maxine Sullivan's pioneering career change? It proved to be merely a sabbatical. She returned to singing in the late 50s and began touring internationally, even coming to France in 1984. The midlife break must have strengthened her, for by all accounts she sang louder the second time around. But certain things never change. Her last recorded performance, made only eight months before her death, was of *Loch Lomond*.

The fiddler had finished his tune to attend to a baby's cry, and the chime of Maxine Sullivan's record, turned now into a distant bell, brought me back to the contemplation of the village through a veil of morning mist. The folks on *this* hill had a view that, sensibly, did not want to be seen so early in the morning. All of those tilting rooftops looked awkward in sleep – like the napping commuter on a bus who threatens to teeter into his neighbour's lap – and I felt almost embarrassed for them as I stared. The place needed more time on a cold morning to wake up and compose itself. Diplomacy decreed I leave it alone and keep heading for the hills.

The village petered out after the Artist's house and the path doubled back abruptly around a scree of grey-white rock. Here the traffic noise from the main road alongside the river below disappeared, as if a curtain had been drawn across the modern world, and the ramshackle sight of civilisation replaced by something entirely primeval: bare limestone crags mooning the sky, trees thrusting out of bare earth, a thick layer of rock shards underfoot. This was the Mer des Rochers, the Sea of Rocks, lapping at the foundations of the ruined castle I had seen the day before. Carving ineffectually through the scrub was a craggy lattice of dry stone walls. A man was sitting cross-legged on one of them.

He made a peculiar sight, this solitary figure atop a wall in the middle of nowhere, yet my earlier non-encounter with the orange-haired cyclist down the hill had steeled me against squandering a new opportunity.

'*Bonjour*,' I said, smoothing together the two syllables in a style I thought persuasively French.

'*Hi*,' he replied, with an American accent. 'Are you Booker's friend?'

We introduced ourselves. Pete had been writing or drawing something in a small black notebook, but closed it to leap off the wall with Fairbanksian panache. He was pale, although a five o'clock shadow had made an early start. Thick black hair was combed back from his forehead into a slick helmet. His face, mercifully free of middle-aged intensity, was smooth except for the thick line of his spectacles, and lower down, the thin line of a pencil moustache, shaved artfully along his upper lip. Here was Clark Kent in a sweater and stonewashed jeans, turning into Clark Gable.

I noted the height of the wall. Where was the ladder? 'That was quite a jump.'

'Nothing to it,' he explained. 'I climb most of the walls around here. When the moon is full on warm nights there's nothing better than coming up to old Roquevaire over there . . .', he indicated the castle looming nearby, '. . . and leaping across a few parapets. But you can't do it if you're wearing a cape in a high wind. What are you doing now? You wanna have a coffee?'

There was already a line of conversation here that needed the company of a stimulant. Perhaps the Clark Kent analogy was not far from the truth. The Sea of Rocks could wait for a sunnier day. In this town, everything could wait.

We retraced our steps down the hill and onto the single-lane Grand Rue, stopping briefly under the lintel of a medieval doorway to make way for a car whose growl was amplified into a roar by the close-set walls. The street opened out onto a *place* with a fountain and a Protestant church. Some of the elders had already taken their usual positions on benches and responded to Pete's *bonjours* with an air of bemusement. Bells over the doors of two *boulangeries* tinkled away as customers exited with their baguettes. A striking blonde woman with a large shoulder bag walked into the post office next to the church. Hers was the only sign of industry in this setting of stasis. No one here looked concerned about being caught doing nothing.

Bordering a side street next to one of the *boulangeries* was a café with a small number of sparsely populated outdoor tables. Several unshaven men who didn't look the *bonjour* type nursed cigarettes in the doorway. I looked at the name on the awning: Café du Commerce.

Booker's story of yesterday. The place where no pig is safe.

I walked towards the entrance, but Pete motioned me on. We continued around the corner of the post office and arrived at another café with the less mercenary name of Café du Jardin. Just as the competition up the road showed little sign of commerce, this place boasted no garden, but there was a terrace with a view back to the hills from which we had descended.

Pete greeted everyone in English.

'Still grappling with the language, huh?' I asked sympathetically.

'Look, I'm a pictures guy. This language stuff is hard for me. It takes time.'

'How long have you been here?'

'On and off – about seven years.'

We found a table away from the fug of cigarette smoke, where the mystery of his parapet leaping and cape wearing was revealed.

He opened his black book. Inside were images drawn meticulously in pen, panels filled with landscapes, streets, arcades and alleys, portraits of fellow café habitués; a modern version of a medieval Book of the Hours, those small hand-painted and illuminated volumes intended for a readership of one. The draughtsmanship was stunning, using the visual language familiar to anyone who reads comics: crosshatching, lines signifying movement, word balloons. One almost expected to see stories about superheroes, or the antics of talking mice. Instead, this was a diary of Pete's observations of his adopted home, depicting the commonplace and making it unique.

'Some of these might turn into big paintings,' Pete explained. 'The rest are just for me.'

The idea of lavishing such care on something that most likely offered no prospect of material gain was a revelation to me. I thought it would also be a melancholy truth for him. But there was, indeed is, nothing melancholic about Pete, who seems the antithesis of the artist as a tortured soul. He exudes a sense of classic mid-Western simplicity, supported by a blithe refusal to engage in materialism. Living rent-free, he shuttles back and forth between his parents' home in Green Bay, Wisconsin, and a small house here in the village, whose owner and friend is proud to have such an exotic tenant setting up an easel in the kitchen directly off the street. (Any passer-by can stop to check on the progress of the latest canvas by peering through the glass panelling of the front door.) Formerly an established comic book artist in the US, working both in the underground scene and on more mainstream fare such as Marvel's *Superman* and *Spider-Man*, Pete now eschews regular work for the more tenuous life of an itinerant painter, preferring to live – as he describes it – 'under the radar'.

He is fascinated by some of pop culture's heroes, and one in particular: Zorro. Indeed, Pete must be one of the world's leading experts on the fictional Mexican. His Zorro collection is immense, filling much of his house with posters, books, original editions of the stories by Johnston McCulley from the 1920s, an archive of the Disney television series from the 1950s – even tracts on swordsmanship.

And the costume.

Now and then Pete opens the French windows of his kitchen studio to leap out into the street wearing the black pants, sash, satin shirt, hat and mask of his idol. (This explained the moustache and dangerously aerodynamic cape.) Clutching his sword, Zorro dashes around the streets, saluting lovely señoritas, placating children and alarming the neighbourhood dogs before heading for the castle overhead. Fearless? You bet!

The locals are accepting of these periodic appearances of Pete's alter ego. Even a daytime flash of black outside the local schoolyard causes barely a murmur. Far from marginalising him further, Zorro has proved Pete's most lucrative link with the outside world. He had just returned from an all-expenses-paid Californian expedition that involved dressing up and sword fighting with a wealthy businessman.

'Was it like playing golf with the boss?' I asked. 'I hoped you let him win.'

This place was becoming ever more intriguing. Multistorey basements, jazz collections in goat sheds, seas of rock, and now my first real conversation with a 'local' who turned out to be an expatriate Zorro consultant. It all added up to something that may not have been definitively French, but was certainly unusual.

So too were some of the hill's other folks who arrived with the approach of noon to take up what were obviously their customary positions in the Jardin. Some of them I recognised from their cameos in Pete's book. My antennae, by now alert to idiosyncrasy, twitched in all directions, forcing me to consider whether this was a stranger bunch than normal, or if it was in the nature of small places to make people's inherent strangeness stand out in sharper relief. Perhaps, being used to the grey anonymity of cities, I was confusing strangeness with personality. One thing was certain – you look at a person differently after having first seen their face in a drawing. The artist's view of his or her subject skews your own, and the readjustment takes time.

A short man in his early thirties with wispy hair hobbled in, tight shorts and a singlet over his compact frame. His vacant eyes avoided direct contact, but he was sociable, and attempted to shake hands with everyone in sight, rasping his *bonjours* in a toneless, smoke-cured voice. Several declined the greeting. I soon understood why when my proffered hand was crushed in his welcoming grip. Nor did he let go.

He muttered something to Pete about Johnny Weissmuller and photos, followed by much slapping of shoulders, and limped down the street, hand outstretched like a politician. Around here, maybe he *was* a politician.

I massaged a hand made tender by bonhomie.

'That's Johnny,' Pete explained. 'He was dropped on his head as a baby. He has this thing about Johnny Weissmuller and always asks me to find him more old publicity shots when I'm back in the States.'

'You mean the guy from the Tarzan movies?'

'Tarzan, and then Jungle Jim on TV. Someone told me he ended up shaking hands with visitors in a Las Vegas nightclub.'

'In that case, your Johnny is a chip off the old block,' I said. Here was proof of the triumph of American popular culture: a French villager sending Zorro back across the Atlantic to pick up Tarzan pictures.

The tables on the terrace continued to fill with people clutching bread and croissants. Some were aprés-Johnny, shaking the blood back into their hands. The clouds cleared and the air filled instead with the sound of the café's jukebox. A clamour erupted at the bar as voices were raised above the heartfelt wails of Johnny Hallyday who, despite being rich and pushing sixty, was calling plaintively for somebody called Marie. Rock and roll Johnny, revered as France's answer to Elvis Presley, is famous for literally rolling (as well as rocking) around the stage of the Paris Olympia in 1960, electrifying an audience accustomed to more vertical performances.

A late middle-aged man at the next table held a thin cigar while speaking such impeccable French he could only have been a foreigner. His two female companions listened with such obvious admiration they could only have been French. Visitors to France are always warned about the intolerance shown by locals to those who are ignorant of the language. This is true to a point; their chilliest *froideur* is reserved for tourists who *refuse* to speak French; or worse, confuse French with loud English. Those who are plainly incapable, such as Pete, are always granted an indulgence. The converse of this is the respect accorded to foreigners who speak at a higher than everyday standard. These days, the genders of nouns so confuse the French that they flummox hapless contestants on television quiz shows. When a foreigner gets it right, they earn a smile of appreciation. Conjugate correctly, and you are up for a standing ovation. An Australian friend of mine who has lived in Paris for more than twenty years completed a post-graduate arts degree at the Sorbonne by writing a thesis on twentieth-century French literary criticism. Her Parisian friends send their children around to have their written French grammar exercises corrected.

The Professor, now our cigar-smoking companion, had retired from teaching German literature at Oxford when offered a generous redundancy package by the British Conservative government and used the proceeds to buy properties in France and Italy. I noted that his English was at least as good as his French. Surely, his German and Italian would be equally polished, guaranteeing him applause through much of mainland Europe. He busied himself researching the history of the village for the local Tourist Office, situated in a small concrete block directly in front of us that I mistook initially for a lavatory. He also took a vigorous role in local affairs, helping to organise some of the annual festivals and keeping track of council expenditure. This had been necessitated by a recent *scandale* that culminated in the imprisonment of the mayor for building his swimming pool with money set aside for the local hospital. Almost as heinous, I thought, as disguising a tourist office as a toilet and putting it next to a pub.

'The locals quite like it there,' said the Professor. 'Most visitors can't find us, and those who do are usually about to leave.'

An emaciated, nervous man asked to join us in a quavering voice. Sitting down, he produced a pipe from his trouser pocket and unfurled a small sheaf of drawings. This, it turned out, was the Artist. I complimented him on his sign and was silently grateful for the fact that we were meeting on a café terrace. It made a better first impression than being discovered under a balcony.

He was an escapee from London. 'I had to get out. One day I realised I just couldn't stand it,' he explained. 'Too much pressure, too many people.' He lit his pipe. 'In the end I think I had a bit of a turn. My wife is a translator who can work from anywhere, so we came here to help me relax.'

For a person released from pressure and British winters into the Languedoc sun, he didn't look nearly relaxed enough. Wherever he went, his disposition would follow, as I knew only too well; I had unpacked mine earlier that morning. At least he could worry with a dress circle view in one of the more salubrious parts of town. His sign was in great shape. I couldn't be sure of drawing, but translating obviously paid.

The Artist asked what had brought me here. Replying that I had followed a friend would sound aimless, and to attribute my journey to an urge to escape, although the probable reason why we were all sitting here, would sound trite. Both were true, but truer still was my twitch of restlessness on the threshold of middle age. I thought about Jimmie Lunceford and his Orchestra and dropping dead at forty-five.

'Actually, I came here to swing.'

'To *swing*?' Glances were exchanged across the table. Johnny Hallyday had given way to Vanessa Paradis.

'Nothing kinky,' I added hastily. 'Just to swing, like . . . like jazz. Find a good rhythm. Play a better song.'

The Professor translated this to his companions, who looked puzzled. I would have had more credibility dressed as Spider-Man.

'And to learn,' I concluded. 'I'm travelling to get my head around something new.'

'People never learn a sodding thing when they're travelling,' said the Artist. 'If they did, tourists wouldn't behave like such complete idiots.'

'*Hey there*, Aline,' Pete called out. A woman in the street with leonine dark hair nodded to us with a cool regard. She wore a clinging lacy top and a short maroon skirt over strong black-stockinged legs, a natty picture of middle age at its most confident. Moreover, this gal looked *healthy*. Far too healthy to be French. After scanning us all with green eyes, she walked on.

'That's Aline Crumb,' Pete explained without prompting. 'The Crumbs are the main reason why I'm here.'

My landlord and his wife appeared to be founders of a colony. Soon I would have to investigate who this Crumb was.

'Well, I'll tell you why *I'm* here,' said the Artist. 'The midday bell has just rung. Anyone else for a drink?'

The ensuing hour passed predictably. I paid for Pete's drinks and retired to the basement for a siesta. By the time I awoke and completed the delicate journey down to the floor from my bed, it was time for dinner. The Professor recommended a restaurant at the base of a medieval watchtower where a string of multicoloured light bulbs lined a wooden platform outside the front door that abutted the Grand Rue, allowing any stray whiff of car exhaust to mingle with the bouquet of the house wine. The glowing reds and yellows, modest as they were, matched my mood of quiet celebration. Day One, and I had already met some locals. They weren't French, but it was a start. I drank a solitary toast to adventure and savoured my first mouthful of the *plat du jour*, sautéed veal with rice. With a soft *crack!* a single flinty grain split one of my molars in half.

FOUR

JUNK MAN

JACK TEAGARDEN AND HIS ORCHESTRA,
CASPAR REARDON (HARP), NEW YORK, 1934

BOOM-BOOM! Somebody was striking up the rhythm in my vanishing dream. It was a knock at the door. I groped my way to the living room window and swung the shutters open to the clearest morning yet of my sojourn. A familiar van was parked by the river. Booker, looking dapper in a cravat, peered up from below. He was back from his road trip to Britain and planned to try the morning's flea market in Alès.

A coffee at the Jardin later and we headed north through the Gard, mountains to our left and rolling hills of vines to the right, their tendrils shooting into the morning sky. Now and then a car would appear from nowhere, hovering inches away from the van's rear bumper, before pulling out and accelerating sharply as it overtook us in a roar of house music and over-revving. One daredevil almost collided with an oncoming car.

'I can't understand why it's necessary to tailgate someone in the middle of nowhere! It's the national pastime,' Booker exclaimed. Other phrases were more pungent.

'How was Wimbledon?' I asked.

'Not the great success I was hoping for,' he admitted. 'A few big collectors must have died this year. When that happens their wives decide to clear the records out from the back of the house to make a few quid on the side. You should have seen the anoraks rubbing their hands together at nine o'clock that first morning. There was plenty on offer, but nothing of much interest to me.'

'You must have enjoyed being back in the Old Dart again.'

'Not really. You see, I haven't lived there since I was about twenty-two. I can't relate to the place any more. I can't even understand what they're saying. Nobody in London has any consonants these days. It all sounds like Cantonese to me. The only upside is looking at the women.'

'You don't enjoy looking at women here in France?'

'Of course, but once you cross the Channel it feels like you've waded into a different gene pool. I've travelled up there a few times with Crumb. Sitting on the London Tube with him is quite an experience. You know he's partial to a certain robust body type, and he has these thick glasses . . .'

My landlord was still a mystery to me. I had yet to set eyes on him, or even present my first rent cheque. He wasn't the sort of guy to sniff around the basement door with his hand out. All I knew so far was that he was an American comic book artist, a friend of Booker and Pete's who was responsible for them both living nearby, and that he had two main interests: old records and sex. It was therefore no wonder that the female passengers on the Tube, so much more upholstered than those on the Paris Métro, would have been as exciting for Crumb as the flea markets in which he and Booker spent time riffling through battered recordings of jug bands.

Alès (population 40,000) is an appropriate setting for a flea market. Situated at the midpoint of the route between the Auvergne to the north and Nîmes to the south, it looks like it was picked up cheap in an Ugly City sale. The place might have been more elegant in the late Middle Ages when it was a centre for silk and draperies, but by the nineteenth century coal mining had become the major industry. After the Second World War, the local government razed much of the medieval city heart to make way for Soviet-bloc style apartments for the workers. It is a feisty and unsentimental town that has no compunction about chucking old things away.

And here was a profitable form of disposal – an expanse of rugs, trestle tables, small tents and vans parked by the river, sprouting a forest of furniture, bric-à-brac, clothes, automobile parts, the innards of obscure, long-superseded and inoperable electronic gear, dismembered dolls, pre-loved girlie magazines, badly tarnished family silver glinting just a little in the morning sun; unloved, melancholy things too shabby for an antiques dealer and too valueless for the pawnshop. Many of their custodians looked like old hands, quick to catch the eye of a passer-by who lingered over a battered pearl-handled knife, or ready to talk up the glorious provenance of a chipped milk jug. Others had simply shovelled out the contents of the dilapidated barn at the back of their property, and sat impassively with their book or plate of cooked pigs' trotters, waiting for their selection of rusted garden tools to sell itself.

Booker knew this terrain well and stepped out of the Kangoo in a fine mood. A born collector, he has the same sort of renewable optimism as a gold prospector, toiling patiently through mud in search of the telltale fleck of gold. But unlike prospecting, sifting through a flea market presents a double challenge: finding the gold, and then persuading the owner to part with it. Booker said that one never knew where or how the next treasure would turn up. He found some of his prize items in out of the way places such as junk shops in small Australian country towns and Oxfam shops in dour London suburbs, but the weekly markets that stud the Gard in places like Nîmes, Anduze and Alès were often a good bet.

He visited them every couple of weeks, keeping a mental inventory of who shifted their wares quickly or slowly, who would negotiate, how often various sellers set up their displays. 'One has to approach this tactically,' he said. It was too obvious to be a bird of prey, swooping down from nowhere, for a canny *exposant* could sniff the buyer's urgency and demand a higher price. A subtler act involved pretending to stumble inadvertently across the object of desire, behaving as if it were of only peripheral interest, mixing a degree of feigned ignorance with indifference. This required a first casual reconnaissance over the hunting ground.

Booker cruised by a table on which 78s were crammed into cardboard boxes, and sidled back to my observation post next to some near-death saucepans.

'Mission accomplished,' he said.

'What have you found?'

'What looks like a good pressing of Caspar Reardon, the only person ever to swing successfully on a harp. His day job was as a classical player in the Cincinnati and Philadelphia Orchestras, tinkling out Debussy with Stokowski or whoever, but he did some moonlighting on the radio playing jazz under the florid pseudonym of Arpeggio Glissandi. In 1934 he got together with the great trombonist and bandleader Jack Teagarden for a couple of studio sessions.'

'The harp? Does it work in swing and jazz? The harp is so . . . *angelic*. Jazz has to sound a bit grubby.'

'Point taken. It helps to be able to slide the pitch around notes, and that's impossible on the harp. But then, the piano can't do it either, and that never stopped Duke Ellington.'

We made a circuit of the rest of the market, during which Booker noted some 1920s magazines featuring photographs of trans-Atlantic ocean liners, and then strolled again by the old records. Booker's bartering technique was flawless. He worked his way through some decoys, getting excited about Cab Calloway, dropping just enough wrong information to convince the seller that he was more an enthusiast than an expert, and was therefore likely to overpay. He agreed to the price quoted without demur. A quick search of his wallet revealed that he did not have enough to take the Cab home. Ah, well – he would try again when he had more ready cash. Perhaps next week.

Lingering over the boxes before strolling away, Booker flicked diffidently through a few last records. He stopped at one, remarking to me in a casual aside that his sister was a harpist. She might find something as outlandish as *Junk Man* to be a bit of fun. The price scrawled in pencil on the paper sleeve was optimistic for an item that nobody else would have reason to buy, but he might as well offer what he had. She was his sister, after all. And didn't he now remember that Cab Calloway selection he'd seen in Nîmes? That market was happening again in a couple of days . . .

The deal was done quickly. Caspar Reardon's *Junk Man* was going home to the Treatment for the princely sum of one euro.

One of the hazards of being an expatriate – especially one living in a part of the world as mythologised as the south of France – is that complete strangers tend to roll up at your doorstep at the urging of allegedly mutual friends. I have always made it a policy never to inflict myself on people on the basis of such a dubious recommendation. But just before I left this time, a friend told me a particularly alluring story of an old school chum who had upped and run off with a scruffy Irish painter. She would pass on my particulars to this exotic pair who would be waiting to stun me with the warmth of their welcome. They lived in a former silk factory in a village 'somewhere down your way'.

I remembered my pledge made years before to seek out the company of eccentrics. This couple sounded to me like perfect candidates, so I mentioned them to Booker as we drove back from Alès. He was euphoric after scoring at the *puces*. Caspar was propped up on the seat behind him.

'What's the place called?' he asked.

'Cardet,' I replied. 'Apparently, it's somewhere down this way.'

'Never heard of it,' he said. '*Spain* is somewhere down this way.'

We stopped at an intersection. A sign pointed to the left. It read *Cardet – 5 km.*

'You should get out more,' I said.

Within minutes the Kangoo trundled past an empty square. It was so quiet that Booker slowed to a crawl as a mark of respect. A bar full of people stopped talking and turned their heads in unison to follow us as the van rolled by. There was a public phone box behind the small church.

A wary voice came on the line. I looked at my wristwatch. It was comfortably late in the morning. Lunchtime, in fact.

'Hello – is that Meg?' I enquired delicately. 'My name is Christopher. I gather you've been expecting me. Well, I made it. I'm here!'

'Never heard of you,' she answered.

Marvellous. I was now that dreaded thing: The Uninvited.

Meg took pity on my obvious embarrassment, and we agreed to meet in the square for an appraisal. She would be the one with a dachshund. Booker and I knew that if the dog attacked it would not be a propitious sign. A large alsatian guarded the doorway of the bar, ready to join any flesh-tearing action. It was probably the dachshund's best friend.

Returning on foot to the square – pausing only to make friends with the alsatian – we spotted the small dog with a petite, dark-haired woman at the other end of his lead. Luckily, we received a canine lick of approval and were invited back to the house. As we stepped through the front door, Booker noticed an upright piano against a wall.

'May I?' he asked, flexing his fingers in a masterstroke of ingratiation.

'That would be wonderful,' said Meg. 'It was only delivered ten minutes ago.'

Booker sat down and lifted the lid. He played a few soft chord progressions, sketching out a harmonic frame much as one might draw the rough outline of a tree before filling in the detail of the leaves, and launched into a fast stride version of *Honeysuckle Rose*; right hand decorating the melody while the left hand pumped rhythmic life support back and forth across the octaves. I marvelled at the way that left pinkie always hit the target at the extremity of those leaps. The great stride piano players like James P. Johnson, 'Fats' Waller and Art Tatum could do this at amazing speed. Booker's aim was just as true, and the sound of the upright filled the room. His body was quite still, apart from the precision movements of his forearms, but there was no doubt about it – he was swinging. Life and joy ricocheted everywhere. The dachshund barked. Sunlight danced on a white tabletop in the courtyard.

'What the *fuck* is going on?' A lanky man wearing a cap over his bald head walked in on the impromptu recital. His brogue made the question sound more hilarious than indignant.

'Micheal, come and meet these people. I must ring Australia and find out who they are,' Meg said, heading for the phone and what I hoped would be confirmation of my identity.

'Hello – it's Meg,' she hollered through the wall of sound. 'Two men came here this morning saying I should know them, and now one of them is playing the piano.'

'What's his name?' asked the friend.

'Booker, I think,' Meg replied.

'Never heard of him. Whoever he is, he's a good pianist.'

'The other one is called Christopher.'

'*Christopher*? He's there *already*? Oh, shit.'

'I don't know who you two fuckers are, but you're coming to lunch,' announced Micheal. 'We're celebrating Meg's birthday. The piano is her present.'

Micheal Farrell, being an artist – and as I was to discover, one of Ireland's most important contemporary painters – was inured to situations like this. If there was one thing I noticed about artists on this trip, it was that nothing surprised them. Pete had barely raised an eyebrow when confronted by a stranger in the middle of nowhere; Micheal addressed himself to our sudden appearance on his wife's birthday as if it had been pre-ordered and served to him in a restaurant. And now, five minutes after setting eyes on each other, we were *going* to a restaurant. Perhaps artists feel that life is all about delivering strangers to your piano to interrupt your work with *Honeysuckle Rose*. I was still so conditioned by the routine of my 'normal' life that the speed of this rapid progression from invasion to celebration made me giddy. (It could also have been the birthday champagne that Micheal served on the spot.) Here was another daily life lesson for my Diploma in Swing: take the hand of the unexpected. To lunch, if possible.

The walls around us were a gallery of Micheal's work. A recumbent bishop, wearing nothing but his mitre and a prayerful expression, received a devout blowjob from a young woman. Pablo Picasso made shapes with matchsticks for an amused James Joyce in a café. The largest painting in the room showed the village square of Cardet in winter, its bare trees ringed by a low wall and lines of house frontages brown and grey in the cold. Two rays of light sliced through skeletal branches into the gloom, suggesting hope and nostalgia without sentimentality, an indulgence for which Micheal had no time. He had been living with cancer of the jaw for thirteen years – nearly a quarter of his life. The cap on his head covered the side effects of his latest course of therapy.

We drove to a place in nearby Anduze and took a table outside that faced the foothills of the Cévennes. I looked forward to trying some true regional cuisine, imagining a family business with rubicund *maman* cooking in the kitchen. Instead, the owners were a Dutch couple, and the cuisine

Indonesian. It was execrable. With my broken tooth I could only chew on one side of my mouth. It took me twice as long as the others to get through the meal.

'If I'd wanted *shite* like this I would've gone to Jakarta,' Micheal said to the waiter, forgetting for a moment that it was he who had made the reservation. 'You should be fuckin' payin' *me*.' I noticed that we were the only patrons, apart from some other Dutch couples.

But the taste of the meal was ameliorated by Micheal's story-telling. He and Meg first came to Cardet on a whistle-stop visit while investigating her family history – a distant ancestor had lived there – and had stopped for a pint at the bar. The place appealed to them instantly after a wet and difficult year living back in his native Ireland. They wanted to return to the sun.

Was there anything for sale? he asked the locals, after shouting everyone a round of beer. Micheal's raffish appearance and excellent French (he had lived in Paris since 1970) demonstrated he was not a typical tourist. A farmer took out a set of keys and showed them the near-derelict property a few doors down from his own.

A deal was done. They moved into the one habitable bedroom with a kitchenette on the first floor, making forays downstairs to shovel out strata of dried manure from the years of holding livestock. The top floor was converted into two big ateliers, one for each of them, for Meg is an artist as well. Five years after moving in, she and Micheal married in the square with most of the villagers in attendance. All this history came from a drink in a bar; but then, hadn't we just enjoyed a birthday lunch with two new friends because of a road sign and an upright piano?

'That was a good story about how Micheal and Meg found their place,' I said to Booker later in the van. It was mid afternoon, and post-luncheon siestas had cleared the roads.

'More than a good story; it's the only sensible way to buy houses around here.'

The conclusion was obvious: if you walked into a local real estate agent wearing expensive clothes and speaking no French, you deserved to pay the ridiculous price posted in the window. One had to stay away from those places, dress plainly, and find a trusted local intermediary who did not work on commission.

This explained how Booker's landlord had picked up *his* place, despite being American and at the time almost mute in the French department. There was, moreover, a further twist in the tale.

It was another link in the daisy chain of association. The

Crumbs lived in California with an increasing lack of enthusiasm. They had friends who lived in a cute French village. Aline Crumb, an incipient Francophile, came over to visit and succumbed to its charm during lunch. She returned with her husband in tow and he reacted the same way. Hearing of a house for sale, they went around for a look. The old woman who answered the door looked surprised (not an artist, obviously) but let them in anyway. The configurations of the place were perfect, with studios for each of the Crumbs and room for their daughter. It was big and rambling and 800 years old, with a great view over the river and a multistorey basement. It called out to them. Intoxicated, they said they would take it.

The owner of the house looked even more surprised. Her house was not for sale.

The Crumbs had knocked on the wrong door.

But on reflection, the woman began to warm to the idea. She was getting on; the house was becoming difficult to maintain. The offer was there. Who knew when such an opportunity would come again? *Voilà* – the Crumbs had their house. Apparently, it cost the equivalent of several of R.'s sketchbooks.

From this house purchase that began as a case of mistaken identity, their property holding had expanded to include the stone goat shed that Booker rented, into which he now carried his black treasure from the morning's market.

He had not overstated the size of the place in his letter. There were two rooms, one above the other, connected by a flight of stairs. On the ground floor a sink and stove jostled for space with a shower, toilet and an upright piano. It would almost have been possible to use all these amenities at the same time. Upstairs was more open, even with the Crumb signature carpentry inclusion of a high-platform bed. A couple of rugs on the floor and curtains of lace hanging in the small windows cut through the thick stone made the place feel cosy. Any medieval goat would have been happy here.

'I find it very comfortable, although the first winter was bitter,' he said. 'I stayed in bed all day and only got up to go and buy croissants.'

After opening a bottle of red wine, Booker fired up his turntable to test whether *Junk Man* sounded as good as its surface had looked. The hiss from the groove as the stylus dropped into place could be reduced by the Treatment. Any distortion, caused by the gouging of old styli, was minimal. The record was in good shape. Booker had not blown his euro on a dud.

Brass intoned some dolorous chords. A clarinet complained up high.

'That's Benny Goodman on the edge of celebrity,' said Booker. 'He's just a year away from his band wowing the young dancers at the Palomar Ballroom in Los Angeles. Swing was about to become *the* popular music in America. He's playing here with the Jack Teagarden Orchestra. Teagarden was a great trombonist, but this is Caspar's track.'

The harp swung comfortably into the sound picture, accompanied by a strolling plucked bass and shuffling snares. Poor Caspar Reardon was yet another of jazz's early casualties, dying in 1941 at the age of thirty-three. Were he still plucking away like this in some Elysian field, he would be one sassy angel.

Junk Man was a triumph, found among some junk in the south of France, in a day of happy accidents. With such a vibe in the air, I was glad Booker had stuck to the speed limit.

FIVE

BRISE NAPOLITAINE

GUÉRINO ET SON ORCHESTRE MUSETTE, PARIS, 1933

THE WIND BLEW R. CRUMB into my basement one day. I had ducked up to the Jardin to savour the flawless sky and spring breeze over a midday snifter. With luck, I would be in time to see the *factrice* as she passed on her delivery round. She was the most popular ambassador for the local postal service in living memory. Perhaps this was due to her care in handling even the most common junk mail, or her charming manner when appearing with a special delivery package. More likely it was the rocking motion of her hips under her shoulder-slung mailbags as she walked uphill.

Whatever the cause, confidence in the postal system was reinstated. More than this, social routines had changed. Some of the café regulars were now either late for the noon drinks or missed them altogether. They preferred to wait at home for their mail and offer a private token of gratitude to the messenger. This also prevented others from inspecting the handwriting of the addresses, as it was rumoured that many with few or no friends were sending letters to themselves. Some of the envelopes looked suspiciously empty, proving that even the barely literate were getting in on the act. But paperless letters or not, the increase in volume kept the *factrice* on the street for several hours each day, much to everyone's delight. The news that she was married to a member of the National Front seemed to enhance her appeal.

No sooner had I settled back with the expectation of an al fresco idyll than the spring breeze turned nasty. Suddenly, this was not a day for handling empty self-addressed envelopes. Dust, litter and berets flew through the air while nearby houses applauded the chaos with unsecured shutters. This must be the mistral! The prospect of having my visit authenticated by living through a classic source of southern French irritation excited me, before I realised that my basement windows were also exposed.

Gulping down my sauvignon (it was a mere *vin de table*, after all) I leapt up and raced away from the *place* Florian, over the little bridge where the underground arm of the Vidourle surged back into view. Arriving at my front door, I saw that it was open, when before it had been closed.

Stepping inside, I heard movement upstairs. This alarmed me. I had heard that theft was on the rise, and my comings and goings through a doorway next to the river could have been clearly observed from any number of hidden vantage points. The sound of my rapidly approaching footsteps would have been blanketed by the howl of the wind, and the doorway in which I stood was the only means of entry, and therefore, of escape.

Keeping one foot firmly on the threshold with my adrenaline purring nicely in second gear, I craned my head to look up the stairway. The room overhead was strangely dark for such a bright day. Whoever was up there did not want to be seen and had closed the shutters. What to do? If only the post woman were to pass by right now, I thought, I could ask her inside to help me out.

When in doubt, speak. It was a lesson I learned in radio. Trying to conjure authority from the hat of panic, I called out in quavering tones.

'Hello?'

'Yeah?' came a voice from upstairs in a reassuringly tentative tone. This was not an intruder – merely a visitor.

'Hello there,' I called again.

A lanky figure floated down the stairs. Last to emerge from the gloom was a bearded, almost cadaverous face burdened by thick glasses. Huge eyes looked at me without expression. Under such strong magnification, a single blink would be a cinematic event.

'Hi. I'm the landlord,' he said with slight self-deprecation.

'I'm the tenant,' I replied, extending my hand in what felt

suddenly like a maladroit gesture. He blinked – *wow!* – and took it.

'When that mistral comes up, you really have to fasten all the windows,' he explained. 'I thought I'd come down to check if everything was okay in here.'

So *this* was the guy? This shy housekeeper was R. (for Robert) Crumb?

A strong *brise* was possibly the only circumstance that might have brought us together. Crumb was not the sort of landlord to turn up at the door with a candle in a piece of cake and a 'Welcome to Our Village!' note, and I was not the sort of tenant to burst into his house with a sack of laundry, especially now I had learned from his friends Booker and Pete that Crumb – much as he would chafe at the description – was a Famous Person.

They showed me a published compendium of his work that Pete had edited, called the *R. Crumb Coffee Table Art Book*. (Pete knew at least as much about Crumb as he did about Zorro.) It showed two things straight away: 1. Crumb was prolific, and 2. that he had emerged from the 'dark' of the underground comic book scene into the 'light' of modern critical appraisal. I mean, this was *serious*; it was a hardback book. On the back cover, *Time* magazine's Robert Hughes described Crumb as 'the Breughel of the twentieth century'. There were several Breughels, but I took the comparison to be with Breughel the Elder (1525–1569) who made famous paintings of dancing peasants. Next to the quote was a cartoon of strange little figures exploding, rather than dancing, from the crazed artist's head, including what I presumed to be the types of women who captured Crumb's interest on the London Underground. As if to rebut the judgements of Hughes and his ilk, a smaller Crumb beneath glared at the viewer from an armchair, saying 'YEAH, BUT IS IT ART?'(comics being an uppercase world).

Inside, I found Crumb's life, as told by Crumb. Apart from selective biographical detail ('we only tell 'em what we want them to know', as he chooses to tell us), it is a cornucopia of neuroses and sexual fantasies, denunciations of the state of modern American society, a catchy slogan or two (Keep on Truckin'), and a bevy of cartoon characters like Fritz the Cat, Devil Girl, Mr Natural, plus Crumb himself, whose flirtation with LSD as an angry young nerd exploded his head to produce most of these creations in the first place.

I browsed through the bizarre gallery of images, trying to catch up with what so many others knew and admired in Crumb's work, trying to make sense of Hughes' Breughel analogy. While I could sympathise with so many of his obser-vations, Crumb's vision is so relentlessly bleak (apart from the obvious pleasure he derives from collecting old records) that I quickly became exhausted, and hoped that he wasn't walking around the house above my head wringing his hands in despair. Breughel was surely happier than this – witness all those dancing peasants. On the other hand, Crumb's merci-less self-study reminded me more of Rembrandt on a downer. Someone who comes up with titles like *Self-Loathing Comics* or *My Trouble With Women, Parts I and II* is obviously not bursting with self-esteem.

But the man sure can draw. The sheer vivacity of the line undermines some of that heartfelt misanthropy, reassuring the reader there is a part of Crumb that cannot help but pull the rest of him in a positive, indeed life-affirming, direction. For Crumb, that arrow points to the past, when people made their own music on their verandahs, in dance halls, church halls, ballrooms, bars, restaurants; back to the late 1920s.

Developing a sense of nostalgia, especially for the music of one's youth, is always a dead giveaway that middle age has arrived. Under this logic, Crumb can be said to have been old before he was born. He is nostalgic for music from the late 20s, and has been ever since he first heard, in his mid-teens, a 1928 dance band record called *Happy Days and Lonely Nights*, played by Charlie Fry's Million Dollar Pier Orchestra. There is a poignant drawing of a tearful adult Crumb carefully holding a 78, staring with longing at the grooves, asking, 'What happened to this music?'. (Behind him, a small pig on a sofa demands he stop being so 'fuckin' sensitive'.) This is more than Crumb's trademark vulnerability; it is mourning for something lost.

Not lost altogether, though. About four thousand 78s live upstairs in his music room. But Crumb does more than just play his records to keep the music alive. He is a capable strummer of the ukulele and banjo, and spent three years attempting to master the accordion. In the 70s he donned a bow tie to play with a band called The Cheap Suit Serenaders. More recently, an enterprising French record producer threw Booker, Crumb and sundry others into a Paris studio to make a recording called *Les Primitifs du Futur* (The Primitives of the Future) featuring snatches of Crumb talking in French. Crumb maintains he cannot master the language at all, despite taking lessons from Johnny Weissmuller Jnr. Under Johnny's guidance, Robert may forever speak French like a primitive, but as long as he avoids the handshake his drawing future is assured.

Since Crumb's adolescence was overtaken by a version of middle age when he was just sixteen, it stood to reason he would come back to it sooner or later. Think of a gang of pimply teenagers at the back of the bus, *phu-oarr*ing at female passengers. Young Robert was never one of the gang, so he waited until adulthood to ogle in style. Fame in his mid-twenties transformed Crumb into a swordsman with the ladies, but the pen was mightier, and with it he depicted the female body type of his dreams.

He describes her vital statistics in precise terms, almost as if he were designing a bridge. His womanly ideal is almost *built* like a bridge, with thick-ankled legs like pylons, strong enough to support Crumb's weight on lap, thighs or shoulders. When she is prostrate on the ground, her buttocks jut upwards like a podium on which the artist can perch. I presume psychiatrists would have a field day. A couple might even quietly make photocopies. But Crumb is beyond psychoanalysis. When you can spill your guts as well as this on paper, there is little need to repeat the process on a couch. In any case, his fantasies are just elaborate variations on a universal theme. As we all know, some gentlemen prefer blondes.

Crumb knows that the business of putting his 'vision thing' on to paper will discomfit some people. Sure enough, in the film documentary *Crumb* released in 1995, a detractor speaks of his 'arrested juvenile vision'. Certainly, he is shown to take great pleasure in riding big-legged women on piggyback, and often draws them in strange contorted postures (and at least once without a head), but far more damaging 'visions' have been forced upon the world. Crumb invokes the Bible in his defence, quoting Jesus in Mark 4:22 – 'For there is nothing hid, which shall not be manifested; neither was anything kept secret, but that it should come abroad.' In other words, if it's in there – even as a juvenile vision – let it out, baby. *Phu-oarr*.

Many creative artists have been fascinated by puerility. The adult Mozart wrote letters about the fun of farting. Crumb has done some funny farting comics as well. I have a feeling he and Wolfgang might have got along. One day an enlightened director will invite Crumb to design a production of *Don Giovanni*.

I figured Crumb to be a misanthrope and started thinking about alternative laundry arrangements. My only advantage was that I did not know his work well enough to be a sycophant. Crumb, I suspected, despises sycophancy. Back in the 70s the *Saturday Night Live* television show invited him to be a guest host. He turned them down. It would have made him even better known, but 'celebrity' gives him the heebie-jeebies. In the grand scheme of things, Crumb is happiest being crumb-sized.

In his late forties he threw down his lawnmower, packed up his records, cashed in some sketchbooks and moved from California to France with Aline and their daughter, but not before a friend made the *Crumb* film about him. Robert's timing was good. *Crumb* was so successful that any remaining anonymity would have been blown away. (I saw the film some time later. What with the stories of his gothic childhood mixed with real-life bounteous babes and the revelation of his prodigious penis, *Crumb* made me feel like a cross between a psychiatrist and a customer in a delicatessen.)

Booker disputed my analysis of misanthropy, insisting on his innate kindness. 'Robert just wants a quiet life,' he told me. And the village seems to give the Crumbs what they want. Their front door is usually unlocked, because they know that no one in their street would walk through it unless they were invited.

Outsiders are not so laissez faire. When you produce weird art, you have to expect some weird admirers. One demented fan and his Korean wife decided to make an unsolicited Crumb pilgrimage. After flying to France from Flushing, Queens, they caught a cab from Marseilles, arriving at four o'clock on a rainy morning with no money for the $200 fare. 'Oh, Crumb, man, I really fucked up,' the disoriented traveller called up from the street while his wife held the luggage. Crumb, roused from bed by complete strangers, paid the driver and let the visitors sleep the night on his kitchen floor before packing them off back to Marseilles later that morning on the bus.

I noticed it was the dynamic Aline who cut a more conspicuous figure around the place. She worked to ensure that other figures were almost as conspicuous by presiding over the local gym class. Posters for her sessions could be found in windows along the Grand Rue, featuring her strong profile atop unmistakably Crumbian legs. The illustration was Robert's, of course. Was he imagining things? No – those legs were all hers; I checked the next time she strode past the Jardin. Gym dominatrix, living personification of her husband's preferred body type, and – as the *R. Crumb Coffee Table Art Book* shows – an established comic book artist in her own right. Fantasy and reality in a package with strong ankles. Aline Kominsky-Crumb was obviously a formidable woman.

Closing the book, I decided that there was nothing to be 'made' of R. Crumb. It was all too complex. I doubted he could make much of it himself. His philosophy is bleak: essentially, the world sucks. But for all the nihilism, he cares enough to look after his old records – and secure the shutters.

'Bring your stuff up when you have to. Just check if someone's around.'

Crumb and I were discussing the laundry. He had a droll way of speaking, his voice often trailing away at the end of phrases into a soft croak. When he laughed, it looked like a real physical effort, his lips pulled back in a rictus, so that one was grateful for it.

He invited me to come up for some dinner. 'After, we can play a few exotic and obscure 78 records.' Forcing the door open against the wind, he left.

'I met Crumb yesterday,' I said to Pete over *pain au chocolat* at the Café du Commerce. We were sitting at the Jardin's rival establishment to satisfy my hunger for adventure. (In your forties, you should try anything – even a stranger's coffee.) Our croissants came from the *boulangerie* next door, run by a woman who in middle age had adopted a short spiky haircut and bought a Harley-Davidson. Each morning she would make a tumultuous entrance on her wheels, looking like a latter-day Valkyrie.

The Commerce was the haunt of Pete's friend Serge, an Italian who made his living buying and selling movie posters. Most of his small income came from Pete, who purchased all of the Zorro posters at what Pete claimed were exorbitant premiums. Despite his love of profit, Serge was an avowed anarchist. He owned a small house in the village, in which it was said he had seduced countless women. As is often the case with men over breakfast, his appeal as a Lothario was not immediately evident.

'Yeah, Robert told me last night,' said Pete. He sees Robert most nights, plus a few lunches. Their houses are so close that, even without any heroic costuming, he can get over some high walls to the Crumbs' door in almost a single bound. 'He says you're gonna come up to have somethin' to eat.'

'He's great,' I added, just in case Pete, having moved to France years before to hang out with the Crumbs and collaborate with Robert on the *Coffee Table Art Book*, had not yet come to the same conclusion. Great, in this instance, meant 'amenable to guests using the laundry'.

'Oh, yeah,' Pete concurred.

Not for the first time, the form and content of our conversation were approaching Zen simplicity. I attributed this to relaxation, rather than a lack of input. The place was finally getting to me, and in the best possible way. Alone in the basement most evenings, I had even stopped talking to myself, and now found it easy to understand why so many of the older people could spend long days sitting near the fountain in front of us without saying a word to each other. The hush was not confined to our table, however; a momentary stillness had settled on the entire café. Glancing up from my croissant, I saw the blonde *factrice* passing through the square.

'No, really,' I added, 'I didn't think he would be so . . . *easy* to talk with. When you've taken a tour through someone's brain before shaking his or her hand it's hard to think of a good opening line. It's like asking someone what their name is the next morning.'

'You should always ask what their name is the night

before,' offered Serge, whose knowledge of etiquette in such matters was considerable.

I recalled some of the pages of Crumb's cartoons. A thought struck me.

'Pete, if Robert doesn't like the idea of being public property, why did he agree to do that book with you?'

'He needed some cash to install the central heating.'

The cyclist from my first morning reappeared and crossed the square towards us. She dismounted and moved from table to table, kissing cheeks all the way. It was a slow and intricate journey that ended when she sat at a rear table with a man whose only hirsute *accoutrement* was a single sideburn. Something about her was different . . . *mais oui!* Her hair colour; it had changed from orange to red. She was turning into a traffic light.

'Who is that wildflower?' I asked, not without poetry.

'She is an acrobat,' replied Serge after some deliberation, finding the right card in his mind's filing cabinet.

'There's a trapeze and high wire company based in town,' explained Pete. 'They tour all over the world, so you don't see them that often.'

Trapeze? Yet another variation on swing. The guy she was talking to looked similarly lean. A fellow member of the troupe, no doubt. He had probably been holding her ankles earlier that morning. Was it warm out here? My eyebrows grew moist; I had broken into a slight sweat. As Booker would say – *steamy*. Maybe the basement was *too* quiet.

'I know what I'd like to talk to Robert about,' I said.

Great minds think alike. Serge excused himself and headed across the square towards the post office, following the *factrice*. He had to send a letter.

Dinner came with accordions.

The walk between the basement and the house above was precipitous; two steep stairways up a high protecting wall, onto another square (this one in front of the *mairie*) filled with parked cars, and into a major thoroughfare nearly ten feet wide. High windows on both sides flaunted boxes of poppies and lines of drying clothes; a preview of what their owners would be wearing tomorrow.

The corner shop was an exotic cave filled with North African tea, spices and sweetmeats. Sweetest of all was Djamila, the sultry-looking owner from Casablanca, her voluptuous figure crowned by wild black hair. Some hinted at a colourful past back in her homeland; a soupçon of gossip that increased the level of patronage, especially from female customers, who always like to inspect 'colourful' women in the hope of discovering what men see in them. Djamila had closed for the night, leaving her window displays to glow as alluringly as she did.

When I reached the Crumbs' house, their front door was unlocked, as usual. I passed through into a hall garlanded with fairy lights and lined by shelving displaying strange plastic figurines, a fitting antechamber to Cartoon Land.

Following the sound of voices and clattering dishes from a stairwell to my right, I came into a long room with a kitchen at one end and a table at the other. In between lay an alcove dedicated to one of Robert's favourite activities: doing the dishes. He has even drawn a comic about it in which Mr Natural's initial distaste for such domestic drudgery lifts as he works his way with dishcloth and elbow grease through a dirty sink load, washing the blues away. I suspect it is a Crumb version of meditation, akin to Buddhist monks sweeping the stairs.

Aline was there, cordiality now in her eyes, looking as well turned out as always. Next to her was a thickset balding man whom I mistook at first to be the Crumbs' on-call security guard brought in to vet me for the occasion. This was Gary, visiting the Crumbs from Los Angeles. Gary had quickly integrated with the place. To be more precise, he had integrated with somebody called Nini, who was one of the village's four piano tuners.

Gary kept talking loudly, but he lost me for a moment as I conjured a thought bubble above my head, as one sees in a comic strip:

THERE ARE FOUR PIANO TUNERS IN A PLACE THIS SIZE? THERE AREN'T EVEN FOUR PIANOS!
WHY DO THE DIMINUTIVE FORMS OF FRENCH WOMEN'S NAMES INVARIABLY SOUND LIKE BABY TALK?
HOW DID HE GET LAID SO QUICKLY?

'. . . I'm getting the keys tomorrow. Why don't you come and see it?', said Gary.

'I'm – I'm sorry?'

'The place I'm gonna buy. It's just past the *place* Florian off the eastern road.'

Day Four of his visit and Gary wanted to buy a ruined hulk on the edge of town that was something between a garage and a warehouse. All it needed was about 200,000 euros' worth of conversion, and a baby grand for Nini to play with. Things happen fast if you come from Los Angeles. Hopefully they would move the money over here fast enough for Gary to head down to the *notaire* with a deposit. He would have to make some more phone calls. The Crumb colony was expanding.

Dinner was simple – ham, salad, cheese, wine and coffee – as was the conversation. We somehow neglected to discuss the state of the world, or women's rear ends, excepting a couple of lewd but affectionate references to Nini's, which had apparently looked fetching the previous evening when sheathed in leopard skin-patterned tights. I began to think about how pleasant it might be to live here and have one's piano tuned by Nini or Gigi or Fifi. Then again, I couldn't play the piano any more. Neither could Gary, it transpired. The drooling tone of his reminiscence about Nini's rear suggested he had not played there either; middle-aged men never sound so hungry after a meal. Perhaps the 'acquisition' of the out-of-town garage was a similar example of braggadocio, or whatever they called it in LA. Perhaps I was envious.

Robert looked keen to have the dishes returned to the sink. Was he itching to slip on the rubber gloves and dig in? Happily, no – he would meditate in suds when the night was over. We left Gary to discuss real estate with Aline in the kitchen and proceeded to the shellac.

'I've been getting this stuff all my life like some exotic butterfly collector,' he said as we entered a room with a faded, sepia look, like Grandpa's den; the sort of room in which 78s would be right at home. There were some old chairs, a work desk in one corner, and sturdy wood shelves along two walls containing his current collection.

Some collectors buy and hold, so that their holdings become a tumour that escapes from a single room and takes over the house, forcing the owner's evacuation. (I know a collector of vinyl who moved into his garage when there was no longer room in the house for his bed. He would shower with certain records to keep them clean.) Crumb caps his numbers and is careful to release a few sides when new ones are due to arrive. His collection therefore changes in composition rather than size, but the focus is constant: late 20s dance music, early recordings of folk music, string bands, jug bands, early blues. Almost all of it dates up to the year 1930, when Crumb loses interest, and when the music loses (for him) its rawness and integrity. In music at least, he is no swinger. Once it edges towards the mainstream, he is out of there.

'Okay – the subject tonight is the accordion,' Robert declared. This was one of his favourite subjects; squeezebox records accounted for a large part of his collection. We began with the black accordionist Buster Moten and *Moten's Blues,* recorded with his brother Bennie's Kansas City Orchestra in 1929 – the same year that a young Count Basie joined the outfit. (Six years later Basie took it over when Bennie died from a botched tonsillectomy.) Next we heard an accordionist from the Auvergne pumping out a country bourrée with fiddle and cello, and then to Bulgaria in a 30s recording of some fast dance music.

'It took me years to find someone who could translate the label,' Crumb said. 'The player turns out to be a guy called Boris Karloff.'

If it was possible to kick ass while squeezing bellows and fingering keys, Boris was doing it. The crackly sound of the shellac took us back to a time when music had to be goaded into life, not with the flash ease of push-button recording studios or iPods or radios, but squeezed and stretched from bulky instruments by perspiring players – music extracted with effort in small rooms, bars and village halls as people clapped their hands and danced. This physicality somehow ennobled the music, making it more deserving of our capitulation to its rhythm. Had I not been in the room, I was sure that the shy Crumb would have tapped his foot.

Flushed with red wine, I was a candidate for revelations, and here one came: that midlife was a time to understand the greatest pleasures came *not* from a surfeit of a single thing, but from the *frisson* of modest and unexpected combinations. Forget self-help manuals – cookbooks hold more wisdom. And this was a heady mix, sitting with a cartoonist in an

800-year-old French house listening to a Bulgarian dance played on the accordion by Boris Karloff. Where else in the world was Boris playing tonight? Nowhere, except perhaps in the memories of some old-timers in a hamlet outside Sofia.

It was getting late, and Crumb had a date with detergent. 'Lastly,' he announced, 'the Neapolitan gypsy accordionist Guérino Vetese, who became the most popular musette player in Paris in the early 30s. This . . .', and he guided the 78 onto the platter with curatorial care, '. . . is called *Brise Napolitaine.*'

Up struck a waltz fit to intoxicate any *bal musette* dance hall, the soundtrack for every foreigner's idea of France. Booker had surmised that Crumb has one of the biggest collections of old accordion music in the world. Well, this was the right country in which to shop.

After the Neapolitan breeze had blown out, I thanked the Crumbs and made the circuitous return journey to the space under their floor. Up on my sleeping platform, I opened the book of Robert's work to see if personal acquaintance had made me see it any differently. The answer was no. The best artists are indiscriminate in their generosity and put it all out there for everyone. But I did find a strip called *Where has it gone, all the beautiful music of our grandparents?* in which Crumb brandishes a piece of wood, chasing a Bruce Springsteen fan. It is a lament for the passing of the old musical folk traditions, trampled in the onward march of technology and blind consumerism. At one point, Crumb draws a condensed history of music that includes – yes – a panel of dancing peasants.

That night my dreams were filled with the joys of unexpected combinations and the frustrations of untuned pianos.

SIX

KEEP YOUR UNDERSHIRT ON

BEN POLLACK AND HIS PARK CENTRAL ORCHESTRA,
VOC. SCRAPPY LAMBERT, NEW YORK, 1929

Though you'll upset me that's a chance I'll take
Go on and pet me but for heaven's sake
Don't get excited
Keep your undershirt on

ONE EVENING I WAS STROLLING alone through the streets, under a tumescent moon in the clear dark blue sky, when I stumbled inadvertently across an orgasm.

The night was warm and quiet. Some upper-floor windows were open to the air, and I became aware of a series of gasps coming from one of them. At first I thought it to be the whimpering of a distressed baby, or perhaps an elderly woman calling her cat. There are an almost infinite variety of sounds that attach to orgasms; like hors d'oeuvres, they are impossible to identify until presented to you on a platter. Which, in this instance, was the case. About ten feet above my head, a woman was about to have her *petit mort*. Judging from the build-up, it was going to be a *big* little one.

As tempting as it was to wait and see how it would all come out, I took the honourable course and kept walking – albeit on tiptoes. It would have been embarrassing for me if the couple were to hear my departing footsteps in their post-coital languor, though I was once in a Parisian hotel where a woman in a nearby room yelled a running commentary all the way to her orgasm at five in the morning. When the show was very obviously over, I joined some unseen guests in other rooms in a spontaneous round of applause.

My reaction to a distant orgasm resembles that of a health expert discovering the first case of a new strain of influenza: to assume that everyone must be having it. Everyone, that is, except me. My ambitions for adventure in coming to France had not included any sybaritic intentions, save those for having time on my hands and wine in at least one of them. I began to see this was not ambitious enough. The news of Gary and Nini, and the evidence of a stranger's orgasm in the night (maybe I had passed Nini's window) were blunt reminders of the celibacy that naturally ensues when you are doing nothing but contemplating your navel in a Sea of Rocks all day. It was springtime, and sex was abroad. And far from being an isolated example, there was more to come.

The next morning I was taking a quiet coffee at the Commerce when a small car pulled up beside the *boulangère's* Harley. A young man burst from the driver's seat in a state of obvious agitation. (I am being subtle here; he was baying for blood.) He stormed into the bakery, yelling something about disgracing the family, and re-emerged seconds later with the spiky-haired owner – who, as it turned out, was his mother – slung over his shoulder in a fireman's lift. He then dumped her in the fountain, dampening the just-lit Gauloises of some of the regulars sitting nearby, uttered a few parting imprecations, got back in his car and roared off.

There were some knowing chuckles from regulars at the other tables, but the consternation became more obvious behind the bar when the *patron* fled upstairs abruptly, chased by his wife who was screaming accusatory questions. It transpired that the bar owner was receiving rather more from next door than hot buns.

This scandal came soon after the news that the local hairdresser had become one of the Gard's major tourist attractions. A trucker confessed to a travelling salesman in the Jardin that Monique in the salon opposite could be relied upon for some good fun when people like him were passing through. There was no harm in this, he said; she was a healthy, mature, red-blooded woman, and her husband was always away on work. The salesman, having just returned home after another long field trip, crossed the street to hear his wife's side of the story before packing his bags and leaving town for good. There were murmurs of regret up and down the bar; not so much that the peccadillo had taken place at all, but that a marriage should have been ruined as a consequence of such indelicacy. *Indelicacy* is not a word one hears bandied about often in a bar.

True, the world is full of such stories. I am not trying to posit this as a quaint local custom, nor is this the prelude to a morality tale. The people in question were all middle-aged and average, even down to their Harley-Davidsons, and *that* is the reason I found these little histories to be so interesting – even heartening. I was becoming concerned (and one *does* consider oneself a matter of concern at this age) less about the matter of marching through my forties, and more about the mounting suspicion that everybody else was marching more elegantly, acquiring all the good and hoped-for things of maturity, like style, integrity, savoir faire and a certain calm wisdom; whereas I was the slacker at the back of the platoon (I still bit my nails, for heaven's sake). Rather than having it all go by too fast, I was not moving fast enough.

But here among the old ramparts, fellow slackers surrounded me. It was much more interesting to observe the older people in the village behaving like teenagers than, say, the local *teenagers* behaving like teenagers. People over forty have put in the practice. In our hands, the craft of adolescence has been refined into high art (or some very good street entertainment). This makes getting older good, honest work, full of meritorious blunders that become more accomplished with repetition. Somebody once said that life isn't a rehearsal. They're wrong. Midlife brings with it the comforting realisation that we are not yet ready for the performance. And the rehearsal is more fun. You can walk into the scenery, forget your lines and flirt with the rest of the cast. Some – but not yet all – of this I was doing here.

Now that the springtime sap was rising, many of the slackers were forming a conga line. The wife of a town burgher had taken up with the local printer in a situation condoned even by the burgher himself, who was often too exhausted after visits to his mistress in Paris to fan the fires at home. The printer's wife took this turn of events less well, fleeing for consolation into the arms of a certain musician that were already full with both an *accordéoniste* – you will recall the voluptuous Franceline from earlier in the story – and a speech therapist who, by night, was the local women's kick boxing champion. (This caused me to quip that she spent her days fixing any damage inflicted the night before.)

With the risk of so many people coming, going and bumping into each other, the most private place the musician and the printer's wife could find for their tête-à-têtes was on a certain pew in the gloom of Uzès Cathedral. One afternoon the interior lights blazed into life and the couple were caught *in flagrante* by an unsuspecting Japanese tour group. 'V-very sorry,' stuttered the leader. 'Group only here to see high altar.'

An Englishman who had rented in the area for years decided it was time to buy, and rang an agency to arrange some inspections. As chance would have it, the voice on the phone turned out to be that of a long lost old flame. When the pair met to look at the first apartment he noticed that time had deepened her bloom, like a good wine. The sparks from the past were reignited, even though the conversation remained at the level of property appraisal.

They looked over the kitchen. She ran her fingers along the granite benchtops and mentioned that most of the gadgetry would be staying.

'Mmm,' he purred. 'Well equipped.'

She then took him to the living room to check its dimensions. Their eye contact was electric. He caressed the lounge.

'Everything is still beautifully upholstered,' he commented lasciviously.

They stepped up to the bedroom. No sooner had he begun to praise the quality of the pillows than she hurled herself at him. They wrestled each other to the floor and vigorous congress took place near the built-in wardrobe.

The pair continued to inspect properties energetically for the next couple of months. In the end, he didn't buy. She was furious at having put in so much work for no commission and summarily dumped both her client and the job to go and marry the manager of a horse stud, exchanging carpet burns for saddle sores.

Back at the goat shed, Booker was excited. One of his Treatments released on commercial CD had just won a Diapason D'Or, which is like the French version of a Grammy recording award. There was no money in it, but considerable prestige; in the rarefied world of sound restoration, he was now a player. At the moment, though, he was more interested in playing with a tribe of young Swedes who had just moved in next door for the summer.

'These are women of substance,' he enthused, 'unlike the young ones around here who tend towards the anorexic.'

He had expressed concern about French women's careful eating before. Having seen a little local television, I thought he had a point. Weather on television is usually a vaudeville event presided over by wisecracking men sporting a signature wardrobe eccentricity. In France, the weather presenters are often middle-aged women, whose trade-off for exposure is to keep the years at bay with discreet visits to Tahitian cosmetic surgeons and a diet of lettuce and air (all one can afford after a visit to a Tahitian cosmetic surgeon). One evening our *animatrice* turned sideways to point out a low-pressure system coming in over Bordeaux, and we lost all sight of her, except for her well-groomed, disproportionately large head. She was a talking lollipop.

Booker and I had been led onto the matter of relations with Sweden by the song *Keep Your Undershirt On*, which reads more raunchily than it sounds:

> *I always let the girls kiss me*
> *If they like it (and they love it)*
> *After I leave 'em they're total wrecks*
> *Oh baby, I'm just full of sex*

Everything sounds very *oom-pah* jocular, but then, it was 1929. Scrappy Lambert could be singing about a brand of hair oil, instead of making a priapic boast. The real slickness is in Ben Pollack's Orchestra, for the Chicago drummer had a knack for spotting and employing young talent: Benny Goodman, Glenn Miller, Harry James and our *Junk Man* friend, Jack Teagarden. All received valuable early experience with Pollack's band, especially when Pollack moved the group from California to New York in 1928.

'Teagarden plays that trombone solo near the end of the

side,' Booker said. 'Pollack doesn't get the kudos he deserves these days. He gave big breaks to a raft of young players who ended up as stars of Swing ten years later. And I mean Swing with a capital S.'

'You mean Swing, the era? Sounds like a brand name.'

'It pretty much is – or was. Johnny Mercer wrote a song about what a fad it had become called *Swing Is The Thing*. And it was: the time when something arising out of jazz became *the* popular music of America. Purists still argue about whether it was "jazz" or not. Whatever it was, it enjoyed a long run of commercial success: ten years, more or less, when the big swing bands ruled the roost, right through 'til the end of the Second World War.'

'But you prefer the small-"s" swinging.'

'Precisely. The earlier bands, where there's still room in the texture for some individual fast and loose playing. In the matter of rhythm, it isn't how big you are, it's what you do with it.'

'Sounds like the cue for a song.'

'We'll have another one shortly, along with a kir.'

'Maybe you should ask the Swedes to join us.'

'They're already consorting with the local riff-raff. I've tried everything from playing the piano loudly to some discreet preening. Nothing registers. I fear that once you get to a certain age – somewhere around fifty – you become *invisible* to people of another certain age.'

'Invisible like that weather woman the other night?'

'Perhaps not,' Booker mused, unconsciously cradling his small embonpoint with relaxed hands. 'She was palpably not there, being on a French woman's diet. *I*, however, am very *much* here. A better description, then, is *transparent*. The Swedes look right through me. The only time I've been noticed so far was when one of them bumped into me by accident at the *boulangerie* the other day. She asked me if I was "all right". Her expression was too solicitous for comfort. I could have been her injured uncle.'

I studied Booker's unlined face and wondered what he had to worry about. His own gene pool was wrinkle-free. A small bump to the forehead from the low lintel of a twenty-two year old's concern, and he thought he had crossed a threshold. If so, the news had not been passed on to his relevant chromosome. Perhaps his hankering (like R. Crumb's) for 'a quiet life' was also having an effect. It is easier to suspend the perception – and maybe even the effects – of time when you are never quite sure what day it is. If he kept ageing at this rate, when the time came Booker would have difficulties getting himself a senior's card; assuming he would ever permit himself to be registered in any country's social security system. Maybe he could apply in Sweden. They like *everyone* to be all right.

Several days later, Booker celebrated a threshold birthday

with a lunch back at the family home in Uzès. A car pulled up, discharging Crumb and Pete, followed by the driver. She wore a short summer dress patterned in crimson tiger stripes, held up only by a couple of straps across her tanned back. Her bleached hair was cut in a bob, and she wore thick, no-nonsense spectacles, giving her face a studious mien that contrasted with the coquettish look of everything below her chin. I guessed her to be over forty, but the natural compactness of her body ensured she would look inspiring in short dresses for many summers to come.

'Booker – what a delight,' I whispered. 'And this is . . . ?'

'She's my piano tuner.' Here was the famous Nini.

Luncheon drinks began just after noon and continued until nine, with occasional breaks for food. From the sketchy accounts we collected the next day, the conversation sparkled at least until main course, but fell away in quality after dessert. Nini excused herself from the table several times to make telephone calls.

'Who is she calling?' Booker asked me.

'I think it's her guy. He's called Gary.'

'*Gary*? That's news to me. They're always called Roger.'

Nini drove Crumb and Pete home after a late round of *digestifs*. Booker and I waved wistfully as tiger stripes disappeared into the sunset, and I hoped that I hadn't been overzealous in my inspection of them during the afternoon.

We repaired to Booker's music room for final kirs and a hearing of a new acquisition from the *puces*, an early 50s vinyl of highlights from Wagner's *Parsifal*. While the music unfolded ever so slowly, I composed emails expressing undying affection to everyone I could think of around the world – as one does after several kirs. Pressing 'Send' for the umpteenth time, I asked Booker how it was that a village of only 1,800 people needed four piano tuners.

'Alès has one of the major piano tuning schools in France,' he explained. 'And students come from all over the country – Nini's from Brittany. One of the teachers used to run a piano shop in our village. He was able to convince the more attractive graduates to stick around in the area and work for him. She was one of them.'

'It must have been quite a shop.'

'Indeed. It was opposite the Tour restaurant where you broke your tooth. You could eat lunch and watch Nini and other lissome beauties bending over a piano's insides. As the ringmaster of such great entertainment, the boss was popular around the place. He even formed a choir called the *Joli Jeu*. They tried to get me to sing in it once. Apparently, there was a surfeit of sopranos . . . is that a collective noun?'

'No. Just a fact of life.'

'. . . And then one day he announced suddenly he was getting married, closed the business and left town, leaving behind some very disgruntled piano tuners and sopranos. I know Nini was very put out.'

'What was his name?'

'His name? Roger.'

The next morning there was a knock at my door. It was Nini in an even shorter dress, plus a straw hat. She had heard that I was living quietly, but the day was too beautiful to spend indoors. There was a lovely spot just outside the village where the river meandered through a maze of rocks. Did I want to come for a swim?

I was touched and terrified. After stammering my *ouis*, I realised I had enough French left to last me for the next six or seven minutes. As one who had only spoken the language in sporadic bursts over twenty years of visits, I had developed a lumpy vocabulary that anchored me firmly in the present tense. This was fine when ordering food in restaurants (such as the village's only pizza restaurant, where I had impressed Pete by calling for *un pizza!* with authentic Gallic flourish), but not so helpful when it came to the more sophisticated business of retelling one's personal history: what I was *doing* on Nini's own turf would be manifestly less interesting to her than what I had *done*. Nevertheless, I chattered incessantly during the short drive in her car, informing her that it is very warm today, the sky is very blue, I am very pleased to be in France, and . . . well, yes, the day is very warm. She nodded earnestly and raised her eyebrows above her spectacles in feigned surprise, as if my pronouncement about the day was a major discovery. Really, the French can be so polite.

We soon found the spot for our swim. Nini parked the car, led me to a riverbank not far from the road, settled herself on a towel, and took off her top. I was accustomed to this form of sun worship from many hot afternoons on Australian beaches, but for some reason this sudden exposure on a riverbank robbed me of speech.

Conversing with a woman who is even partly undressed is a delicate matter, unless you are the reason for her being that way. Decades earlier I was staying in an artist's house in the hinterland behind Nice. On my very first morning I was awakened by the aroma of hash cookies baking in the oven and a distant sound of splashing. When I sat up in bed and peered through my window, I saw a dreamlike apparition of two girls skinny-dipping in the pool. Later, emboldened by one of the cookies, I approached a still-naked sprite as she tanned herself to ask her name, making a heroic (and only partly successful) effort to stop my adolescent eyes straying from her face. A voice somewhere to the north of my gaze replied, 'Pandora'. There was nothing much to be said after that, either.

Our riverbank was therefore quiet as Nini browned herself in the sun. Art Tatum rippled from the car's dashboard. And then she asked me if I liked singing.

When I *oui*-ed, she told me about the *Joli Jeu*. Faced with an imminent full-length concert in the Protestant church, the choir was in the middle of a recruitment drive – her expression was 'we need men' – and news had got around of my musical interests. (They must have been hard up for gossip at the Jardin now that *l'affaire Monique* was over.) Why didn't I come along with her to next Tuesday's rehearsal? We could have a drink together afterwards. I should meet the new conductor.

'But where is going the old one?' I asked mischievously (if ungrammatically).

Nini glared straight ahead and delivered a largely incomprehensible tirade. Her conclusion was clear, however: most conductors are bastards. I nodded my head in sympathy, concurring aloud that 'many symphony orchestras are feeling the same'.

It was agreed that I would come along to rehearsal the following week. Nini's breasts had been effective instruments of conscription. We drove back to the village, where a glass of wine and what she called a *cigarette spéciale* would be provided in her apartment. I was wary of the *spéciale*, remembering again the artist's villa with the water nymphs, when I reacted to my first ever joint by laughing for several hours at a teapot. But one is always more sincere when stoned, and I reasoned that now Nini had put her clothes back on, my French would improve.

Her place took up the entire first floor of a house with a

double-door entrance under a carved stone architrave. It was cool inside after the heat of the afternoon. There were paintings on the walls; one of them a fetching nude that I was now in a position to recognise as being Nini. The message light on her answerphone was blinking. She pressed the play button to hear them back.

The first one was in English. '. . . I don't know what the FUCK you think you're playing at, but I'm coming round there to spank that little TUSH of yours.' It sounded uncomfortably like Gary, and he was angry. He tried again in the next message, this time more conciliatory in tone, reminding her in West Coast love-speak that 'after the other night, I thought we had something special'.

Nini was preparing her own *spéciale* and telling me that Gary was reading far too much into what was really a simple situation. I didn't want to pry into the situation's simplicity, but I knew it would be awkward if Gary burst into the apartment to discover me laughing at Nini's *cafetière*. I made some excuses in the present tense and left, hoping that she would also get her tush the hell out of there before things got even *more* simple.

The *Joli Jeu* rehearsed in the large ground-floor room of a four-level house on the Grand Rue. Four hundred years ago it would have been the cellar, with its low vaulted ceiling and flagstone floor. Even though it was near the end of April, some embers of a fire glowed in a large hearth, and candles burned on tabletops, windowsills and patches of floor. In such a quasi-medieval setting, we were bound to attack our plain-chant with some good old monkish gusto.

As Nini had mentioned, there were many more women than men, standing around in small groups and talking animatedly in French. My sheepish arrival was not greeted with an abundance of curiosity; perhaps, being sopranos, they would become more interested once they learned I was a tenor. I was steeling myself to chat about that day's tempera-tures when someone tapped me on the shoulder.

'Hi there, *amigo*.' It was Pete.

I had not seen him for a while. Another comic book crony had come to stay and the pair were spending long days sketch-ing and painting in the Mer des Rochers.

'Pete! I didn't know you could sing.'

'I can't. But I heard the cry of a *señorita* in distress. And when people cry for help,' he declaimed heroically, 'Zorro is there.'

'I don't suppose the *señorita* was Nini?'

'Oh, yeah. We were up in the Mer the other day . . .'

Tanning the tits again, I thought.

'Fancy seeing you here.' The Artist joined us, carrying a plastic cup of sauvignon in one hand and a pipe in the other. I glanced over to see several more bottles on a candlelit table. He was making an early start.

'I didn't know there were so many music lovers around town,' I said with relief. There would be some fellow English speakers to huddle with after the rehearsal.

'Oh, I don't do this for the music,' corrected the Artist. 'I do it to be social. It's good for my French. I've been here for years and I still can't get the hang of it.' His voice was tremulous.

'Well, since you're further up the learning curve than I am, remind me what *Joli Jeu* means,' said Pete.

'Pretty game,' I ventured, thinking the name too flippant to describe the serious business of singing in a choir.

'Well, you'll need to be pretty game to sing with this lot,' suggested the Artist. 'Wait 'til you hear them.' His laugh quickly dissolved into a coughing fit and he groped his way to a chair in the bass section, sipping his wine as a curative. One always felt when starting a conversation with the Artist that he might not live to finish it.

Nini led the Maestro over to say hello. Her luxuriant mane of greying dark hair cascaded around a careworn face free of make-up, and her eyes were guarded in their expression. Something about her was *blessé*, Nini had said; she mentioned a painful divorce. The smile, though, was broad, if slightly nicotine-stained. She was not 'pretty', yet her persona exuded a strong sensuality; jeans and a loose top draped over a robust, *sportif* figure that this former equestrian had maintained into her middle age.

The Maestro had been the choir's champion soprano. When the mercurial Roger decamped, she stepped into the breach to become the director, and was still not confident about her conducting technique. I was interested to see how her pullover would tug at her torso when she waved her arms.

'*Bonsoir chef,*' I said, mixing respect with a touch of flirtation. She looked surprised to see so many men. Pete and I were the new tenor section; the Artist and a fellow called Ivan comprised the basses. There were about sixteen women of various voice types, yet despite this imbalance the Maestro wanted us to sing some Russian church music, which normally requires hordes of men with massive testicles. This would be a heavy burden to carry. I suspected it was all up to Ivan. He spoke Russian, which was a start, and he sounded as if the low notes would be in his range. But the *chef* was about to give her downbeat (arms too stiff) and I felt *joli jeu* for the challenge.

A strange caterwauling erupted from the sopranos, engulfing the altos. Pete waited for me to hit a note and then spoke the words underneath. Ivan sounded sonorous. The Artist coughed non-stop into his plastic cup, spraying sauvignon over his sheet music. The music was by Tchaikovsky and our performance captured unerringly that quality so prevalent in his work: an ineffable sorrow. If anything, we ratchetted this up into more of a universal pain. Some dogs up the street started barking.

The Maestro's conducting proved to be a most agreeable sight, particularly when her upbeat was directed at me. But she also knew how the notes were supposed to fit together, and worked to coax a smoother sound from the sopranos. Ivan was consulted about Russian pronunciation. Somebody slipped the Artist a pill. We tried again, and then again. Darkness fell, our shadows became more distinct and flickered on the ceiling, and the music began to move us back past Tchaikovsky to a time when candles lit up all the places along the Grand Rue, back to when middle age happened at twenty. The singing, though still inaccurate, had a sense of purpose this time, and when the last chord died away we instinctively observed a silence to let the feeling linger. Some of us exchanged small smiles in the dim light.

'*Merci*,' murmured the *chef*.

We extinguished our candles, finished the wine on the table and spilled into the Grand Rue to walk down the hill to the Commerce for a chaser. The owner and his now ever-present wife looked on as we bunched up together around a couple of tables with our beers and wines, throwing our languages back and forth. (Small choirs are convivial things, especially when women outnumber the men by four to one.)

Pete and the Artist announced they were busy preparing for the May festivals, when all of the village painters, potters and craftspeople let passers-by have a look through their workshops and ateliers. The Maestro was taken with my compliments about her time beating, although I suggested that for clarity's sake she should raise her arms higher for the upbeat and, if possible, arch her back. (My motivation was more aesthetic than musical, I admit.) Nini asked me in front of the other sopranos to comment on the weather. Spring, I declared, is very warm. This brought the house down; why, I couldn't tell.

Later that evening I stared in the bathroom mirror, uncertain as to whether my reflection would ever again provide me with sufficient companionship on this trip. Internal dialogue was undoubtedly harmonious, but it was also becoming boring, for I never disagreed with myself. There was something to be said for the comfort of strangers, a song and a late drink. This is so obvious, I hear you say; and indeed I had known this at some point in the past, way back in Act One of the opera, when everyone is happily singing and drinking, and before the middle act brings its cross-purposes and crabby ensembles, and we start to look at our watch and wonder how much more there is to go. My revived pleasure in society was, therefore, a small step forward, nothing profound, yet the best adventures often involve the rediscovery of the obvious, rather than the revelation of the unknown. In that respect, it had been my most adventurous day of the trip so far.

Things might have been so different had Nini kept her shirt on.

SEVEN

GET OUT AND GET UNDER THE MOON

HAL KEMP ORCHESTRA, NEW YORK CITY, 1929

Underneath the bright silvery light
You'll be feelin' better soon
Pick up your hat, close up your flat
Get out, get under the moon!

IT WAS NOT A DAY for talking to the swans. Morning ritual evolves quickly wherever you are, and worship of the new day becomes particularly essential for the spirit when practised in a basement. Mine was simple: clamber down the ladder from my sleeping platform, open the window shutters of the living room, look at the sky, and let the fresh air circulate around my nether regions. After a naked stretch, I would bellow a hearty *bonjour* to the two swans and their attendant ducks.

A Saturday in early May, I flung open the shutters to give my pudenda their little moment in the sun.

Fifteen artists facing me from their easels on the far river-bank nudged each other, giggled, and began to mix the appropriate flesh tones on their palettes. Ducking down beneath the sill, I groped frantically for a shutter to close, but the damage, alas, was done. This was the Painters Festival, when amateur Cézannes and Van Goghs from all over the region could set up anywhere, as long as they did not stop the traffic. Now I had given them the opportunity to put a little still life into their landscapes. When I exited my front door half an hour later, looking Garboesque with sunglasses and pout, they were still there, greeting me with a barrage of *bonjours* and wolf whistles.

It was going to be a big *bonjour* day. The preceding month had made me quick on the draw with the word; I had even managed to greet the cycling aerialist a few times, noting how her hair continued to traverse the colour spectrum. I bounded (yes, *bounded*, such was my urge to swashbuckle) up the stairs to the main square surrounding the nineteenth-century town hall. Bells rang, their tolling mixing with the distant sound of a brass band. The day was glorious and clear, and the air shimmied with the euphoria of it all.

Scanning the sharpness of the high ridge etched against the sky, my eyes suddenly watered, less from sentiment than from pain as Johnny Weissmuller Jnr, appearing from nowhere, seized my hand and shook it warmly. '*Ça va*? *Ça va*? he grunted with each downward pump and mash. 'Ah! *Oui, oui,*' I gasped, unable to contain my emotion. Courtesies exchanged, Johnny limped on smartly into the throng of people to continue his greeting schedule.

I had never seen the streets so busy, though the crescendo of activity had been noticeable during the past week as the caravan park east of the village filled up with families whose children bombarded the swans with pebbles, and the car park on the highway side of the Pont Vieux became congested daily with tour buses. The influx of tourists is less noticeable in big cities, with their hotels and convention centres. The people are simply *there*, and in summer there are just more of them in places one can take pains to avoid.

In small places like this, any influx has a tidal impact. There were still no hotels, so visitors were perforce day-trippers, sweeping through the open spaces like a camera-toting pocket tsunami, snapping (do people 'snap' any more? In these days of digital cameras, they just 'squeeze') pictures of the locals hanging out their smalls in high windows – pictures of laundry being a favourite 'we were there' souvenir – or sur-prising the elderly as they walked out of the *boulangerie*. More than a few baguettes were dropped in these ambushes.

I was a visitor too, so had no logical reason to deny others their happy snaps. Indeed, almost *everyone* here was a visitor; according to the Professor, some eighteen nationalities made up the population. From the viewpoint of a Roger, this worked out at about four-and-a-half countries per piano tuner. The proprietor of the shop filled with musical instruments on the Grand Rue, toted as the maker of the finest wooden flutes in Europe, was an Israeli; the woman who painted forgettable pictures of flowers in a top-floor studio came from Iceland; the dentally challenged worker on various farms in the region who spent his earnings at the Commerce was Spanish. The place was a zoo in which nobody realised they were an exhibit.

Still, the waves of tourists rankled, just a bit. The old French residents were probably used to it, but we newcomers were possessive of our enclosures. All this indiscriminate capture of images – this was *pillaging*, dammit! I consoled myself with the thought of thousands of slideshows on computer screens in Kansas City, Rotterdam or Osaka, in which the caption 'More quaint Frenchmen' would accompany images of Booker, Zorro and the Professor ceremoniously holding their wine glasses aloft on the Jardin terrace.

Today was also the annual Floral Festival. The main traffic route into the *place* Florian was lined with window boxes taken from their customary elevated positions and placed side by side on the pavement. People milled about, buying poppies, filling the two bars, waiting for a café table to be vacated. Now and then I spotted a fellow chorister from *Joli*

Jeu leading a child covered in artificial verdure to a meeting point for the child-flowers – or would they be flower children? – from where they were due to process through the village later in the morning before being submitted to the indignity of a costume judging.

A big hand thrust out from the crowd and clapped me on the shoulder. Oh, shite. It was Gary.

Luckily, I had no cause for worry. He was full of good humour. He and Nini must have patched it up, although I reasoned that if she had shown him her breasts, he would be a member of the choir by now.

'*Hey* man . . . why don't you come and see the place? It's just a few minutes down the road.' This was Gary's new French love nest.

'When do you move in, Gary?'

'As soon as it's a done deal.'

'What – the owner's dragging his heels?'

'No, everything's great at this end. I'm just waiting on my cash for the deposit from LA.'

I could hardly turn down Gary's invitation; I didn't want my tush spanked. We threaded through the mêlée and turned into a series of side streets until we reached what looked like a small bombed-out warehouse.

'Obviously, there's some work to do out here,' Gary explained. 'But you can see the potential.'

Seeing potential in a ruin was never my strong point. And this was something less than a ruin.

'Sure – once you clear some of this rubble and get all the walls back up, it'll be great,' I enthused.

'Let's have a look inside,' Gary suggested, pulling some industrial-sized keys out of his back pocket to slip into a metal door. There was actually no need for such decorum; we could have climbed through the gaping hole that had once been a window. Judging by the smell inside, every cat in the neighbourhood had already done so.

'There's quite a bit of work to do here, but you can see the po . . .'

'Yep, I can see it.' All I could see was a place that, left alone for another six months, would complete the demolition all by itself.

'The kitchen will be *there*.' He indicated a far corner where a detumescence of rusty piping hung from a wall. Some shrubbery tested the air through a hole in the floor. 'Living area . . . right *here*.'

'You'll have to make sure there's a roof.'

'Absolutely. And the bedroom will be up *there*.' Gary motioned to a point halfway up the high wall at the rear.

'I'm no expert, but you're right. There's a bit of work to do,' I agreed. It would be like rebuilding Berlin.

'I'm gonna get a couple of guys over from LA to help me out.'

'Where's the piano going to go?'

'The *what*?'

'The piano. At the Crumbs, you mentioned a piano.'

'Oh man, I don't play no fuckin' piano.'

Ouch. I hoped Nini's tush was all right. She would be less comfortable than the owner of this pile who, after doing the 'deal' with Gary, was probably out there now, finalising the architect's plans for the new villa near Anduze.

Still, the Gard was awash with émigrés because such dreams could work. Molly was a *serveuse* at the Tour restaurant and a soprano in the choir. She and her partner Richard had sold their one-bedroom flat in London's Brixton and bought a four-level home in the village, with enough money left over to renovate. I could see the potential in that one. It even had a roof.

Gary was having pizza with the Crumbs later that evening. We agreed to catch up then, and I left him among the potential to amble back to the crowded square, where teenagers stood on the ledge of the fountain for a bird's-eye view of the forthcoming parade. An old couple vacated a small table at the Commerce for the cool of their home, so I quickly took their place to have a beer and let Artie Shaw's *Frenesi* play through my head. Zorro, the Maestro and the Artist stopped by, Booker found the chair opposite, and Franceline embraced her repairman, having given Eric the royal send-off. But you already know this.

'I appear to be enjoying an elevated status in Uzès these days,' Booker declared over the approaching march tune by Saint-Saëns.

'Uh? How so?' His interjection had broken my brief meditation, inspired by the news of Eric's non-musical activities.

'The letterhead.'

'You'll need to remind me.'

'At the end of my unhappy time at the embassy in Paris, during which I suffered various indignities at the hands of a superior whose diplomatic prowess was best exercised on the back seats of government cars, I repaired to the sanctuary of my rented flat with as many souvenirs as I could pocket from a hasty clearing out of my desk. These included a supply of embassy stationery.'

'But that was five years ago.'

'Call it an investment in the future. Well, the other week some roadwork sprang up – or, to be more precise, dug down – outside my mother's house, making egress via the driveway almost impossible.'

'Given that your mother continues to drive as she approaches her nineties, I would have thought that a welcome constraint.'

'She's sufficiently strong-willed to overcome such obstacles. Don't forget, she was in Alexandria during the war.'

'I didn't know there *were* any obstacles in Alexandria during the war.'

'It was still the war. The point is this: she likes to think that she is still mobile enough to exercise her options.'

'And is she?'

'Almost. Last year she announced she was driving to the local wine co-op, jumped into her car, and reversed into the cleaner's vehicle at about forty kilometres an hour.'

'I presume her aim is better going forward.'

'We are *all* better going forward,' aphorised Booker, reaching for his beer. The procession was about to enter the square. 'And I quite like the idea of being able to go forward via my own driveway. So I rang the local authority to ask when the work would be finished.'

'Well, your French is good. I'm sure you did it superbly.'

'Too well, I suspect. They reacted with the telephonic equivalent of a shrug of the shoulders. Serves me right for trying to speed up the operations of the most stubborn and convoluted bureaucracy in the world. Mark my words, if you ever think you want to live here. So then . . .'

'Let me guess; you wrote a letter on some stationery that was handy.'

'Indeed. The French insist on the tedious observance of any and *every* bureaucratic procedure, but they revere status even more. This is the homeland of the pecking order. The letter-head made my complaint look brilliantly official.'

'You had better luck this time?'

'You could say that. Two mornings after I sent the letter, there was a knock at the door. It was an official from the *Département*. He apologised for the inconvenience caused by the roadwork and assured me that it would be completed and cleared within days. And so it was – on schedule.'

'Sounds like business can go back to normal at the local wine co-op.'

'There's more. While we were talking, he called me *monsieur l'Ambassadeur*. Perhaps the cravat fooled him. I considered this to be perhaps *too* dangerous a case of mistaken identity, so I corrected him by saying that, while I was *from* the Embassy, I was down here from Paris on business requiring the utmost discretion. I could see that *monsieur* was also a man of discretion, and his co-operation in keeping silent about this situation would be rewarded by the everlasting gratitude of my government. I whispered this last part into his ear in as confidential a manner as possible.'

'Which would have ensured that word got around.'

'Exactly. Yesterday I was dodging Germans in the Uzès market during one of my rare trips into the centre of town, when I noticed a gendarme staring at me. When he saw that he'd caught my attention, he saluted.'

I lifted my *demi*. 'Well, here's to you – *mon capitaine*.'

The raggle-taggle brass band entered the *place* and blazed its way around the fountain. The crowd responded much as it would had the band been comprised of travelling salesmen (which, on consideration, was more than likely, given the sound they were making. Would they slow down outside Monique's salon?), by raising the general level of conversation, keeping eyes averted from the music's public massacre, and putting fingers to ears when the tuba came within spitting distance.

The floral procession, following in the band's wake, received a more enthusiastic reception. Some of the bigger flowers relished the attention, strutting proudly to the rhythm set by the bass drum just in front. Many of the younger ones were clearly overwhelmed, with several tear-stained poppies calling for their *papas*. A single sunflower came to a halt and started shredding her petals in a tantrum. Her mother scuttled out of the crowd, spanked the botanic tush, and hurriedly led her poppet away to be de-flowered in disgrace.

'You know the problem with that band?' Booker said.

'Let me see . . . they can't play?' I hazarded.

'That's obvious, but not entirely relevant in a situation like this. No, they can't *swing*.'

'They're not supposed to swing. They purport to be a marching band.'

'It would help if they did. Even if people only walk in time, you still have to get them on their feet.'

'Maybe you're being too subjective. Maybe they *did* swing and we just didn't feel it.'

'You saw the impact they did *not* have on the crowd. Believe me, had they swung, somebody would have noticed.'

Yet again I recalled my intention in coming here, one I had discussed with myself many times in my basement and described so clumsily in my first conversation with some of the café regulars. 'I came to swing,' I had said, 'swing' being a metaphor for – what? To answer the question, I would have to go back a step and define swing itself, a task seemingly beyond the capability of the spoken or written word. Writers concur that swing is too elusive a musical element to define, but add helpfully that many people know it when they hear it. Tapping one's foot is a giveaway.* Duke Ellington gave a definition by example in his 1932 recording of *It Don't Mean A Thing If It Ain't Got That Swing*, in which his Orchestra's brass section illustrate their vocalist Ivie Anderson's words with a

Doo-wah doo-wah, doo-wah doo-wah, doo-wah doo-wah, doo-wah doo-wah

like some wild, speeded-up heartbeat. Duke was too busy writing music to be a full-time philosopher, but I reckoned his

---

* e.g. Gunther Schuller, *The Swing Era* (Oxford University Press, New York, 1989).

drift was that whatever put the *doo-wah* in your life was the right thing to do. Even if it was just a fleeting tap of the foot in the moment, one should remember that moment, and work on coming back to it.

At some stage of this holiday morning I *had* felt a *doo-wah*, I was sure of it; but I couldn't isolate the cause or the instant. Was it the thought of *Frenesi*, the sky, the visitors to my table, the crowd, the south of France? It certainly wasn't the band. Just like having a *bonjour* always at the ready, I resolved to be more attentive to the moment should a *doo-wah* come again.

Booker and I decided to take our own refuge from the heat and departed the square to make our way towards his goat shed. He slapped his pockets.

'Shit. I appear to have misplaced my keys . . . ah, yes.'

'You have them?'

'No – but I know where they are. I left them at Nini's last night. Let's go and retrieve them.'

It would have been ungentlemanly to probe for detail, so I confined myself to a general enquiry.

'A pleasant night at Nini's, was it?'

'Superb. Salad, cigarettes, some fine blue Fourme d'Ambert, a cabernet from Domaine Houtier, and a fumbled attempt at Schubert's C minor Fantasy on her upright. It requires four hands, you know. Here we are.'

We knocked on the door through which I had hurriedly departed some nights before, but Nini was not answering; nor did she come to the window when we called up to her first-floor balcony on the other side of the house. Booker began to fidget with irritation as we stood impotently on the street.

'Hey there, *amigos.*'

Zorro rounded the corner. He had been startling some tourists eating their lunch at the Tour restaurant.

'So what are you guys doin'?' he said, Mexico giving way to Wisconsin.

'Nothing, due to circumstances beyond our control,' said Booker. 'I've left my house keys up in Nini's flat, and she's not there.'

Zorro's eyes narrowed momentarily behind the mask. A melodramatic voice chimed in my head. *'Could he too have designs upon our most popular piano tuner? Or is there already a History?'*

Then he relaxed. 'Why don't you let me get them?' he suggested.

'Can you get in?' I asked.

'Just watch.' Zorro walked to the wall under the balcony, seized a drainpipe, and in seconds had climbed up to the first floor and leapt over the balcony railing, his cape swirling behind him. The French windows were soon opened and, after a couple of minutes, a set of keys thrown down into Booker's upturned palms. Another swirl, some understandable grunts (Zorro not being quite what he was) and the figure in black returned to earth. I clapped slowly in admiration.

'No problem,' he said. '*Hasta luego, amigos*. And remember, wherever people need help . . .'

'Zorro is there,' Booker and I chorused.

'*Adios!*' His heels clicked as he hurried down the street and back to the *place*.

The village was quiet by dinnertime; tour buses on their way to Arles, brass players florid and blown out, baby flowers all tucked up in bed. Booker and I joined Gary and the Crumbs for dinner at the local pizza restaurant, another unventilated medieval cellar in the main street. Taller customers had to stoop before sitting at their table, and the combination of cigarette smoke and the pizza oven's heat fanning back from its position near the front door turned the place into a toxic Turkish bath. However, it was the cheapest feed in town, and the pizzas were good, despite the constantly intoxicated state of the owner. His wife sat glumly by the cash register, nodding to us as we took turns to step outside for some deep breaths of fresh air, or to dab at our watering eyes with paper serviettes. All five of the main restaurants here were family businesses in which the husband was also the cook, but this was the only one to present an obviously troubled marriage to the clientèle six nights a week. It felt almost like an affront to discover miserable people in a place where everyone should have been happy.

'The atmosphere here is so poisonous – and I mean that in every way – it's amazing they stay in business,' I said to Booker.

'This is France,' he replied. 'People will disregard ancillary circumstances for the sake of good food, especially when those circumstances are as trifling as the ones here. These daily sideshows of the owners' domestic state are good fodder for bar talk around the place, and the air in here is just like any Frenchman's lung.' He cadged a cigarette from the next table.

Gary talked about the felicities of roof construction with Aline, who was gradually enlarging the Crumbs' own property portfolio. Robert, seated next to me, was not taking part in the conversation, and when I looked over at him I saw that he had produced a fine felt-tipped pen from an inside pocket and was doodling a cartoon on the paper tablecloth next to his plate.

It began as a little single-propeller plane with a mouse-like pilot. Gradually, the outlines thickened with repeated strokes of the pen, and Robert added a cityscape of sky-scrapers, following his imagination as it wandered. The drawing grew in size, so that his pizza was put to one side. When his pen slowed to a halt after some final crosshatches, I waited for the moment when we could settle the bill in the hope of pocketing this unique souvenir. Robert was ahead of me. As he stood to leave, he ripped his latest opus free of the table.

The Crumbs peeled off to head back to their house with Gary, and Booker and I moved on to the new wine bar on the corner of the Grand Rue and a side street. (Narrow it may be, but in a village, most things happen on the Grand Rue.) The proprietors had attempted a contemporary look with their décor, the mottled pink walls harmonising nicely with the complexions of some of the regulars.

We joined the most elegant of the tables, presided over by the Professor, who was discussing Handel's operas with a visitor from Britain. Back in his Oxford days, the Professor reviewed opera productions for specialist music magazines, and Handel – a German who composed successful operas in Italian for the English long before he composed the most famous of all oratorios in English to the Irish – was an obvious passion for him.

I had gone through a *pichet* or two of red wine with my pizza and was feeling cheekily adversarial.

'So, Professor – what *is* it about Handel that grabs you?' I asked, not being sure if 'grabbing' was quite the right description for what the Professor would have classed as a delectation for the mind. But the Professor is a man whose generosity of spirit made him more friends around town than anyone else I had met, so he was happy to engage me at this low level of entry.

'What *grabs* me,' he replied without sarcasm, 'is the quality of the music, and the way it portrays passion, especially in the women's roles. For a composer whose love life seems to have been nonexistent, some of those melodies are so voluptuous – even erotic. You know *Giulio Cesare*, don't you?'

'Yes.'

'Think of that sublime music Handel gives Cleopatra when she sings to Caesar:

> *V'adoro pupille*
> *saette d'amore*
> *le vostre faville*
> *son grate nel sen*

> *I adore you, eyes*
> *Lightning bolts of love*
> *Your sparks*
> *Are welcome in my breast*

The Professor lived half of the year in Lucca, and could caress each syllable with Italianate care, letting his warm voice roll around the room. His skill at oratory was almost music enough. All it needed was Handel.

'Or the moment in Act Three of *Alcina*,' he continued, 'when the sorceress realises that her magic powers won't let her have the man she wants, and she sings "*Mi restano le lagrime*". Handel's music shows you that he knew about the desire, pain and longing inherent in the human condition. He presents us with a basic truth.'

'Personally, I prefer a bit more action,' I said stupidly.

'How so?'

'Well, Handel opera doesn't exactly gallop along, does it? All that externalising of inner feelings takes time. Look at Alcina. There she is, stuck out in the middle of nowhere, banging on about how she feels, what she wants and what she can't have, while everyone else just stands around waiting for the plot to resume. I know it's opera, so I don't expect naturalism, or even plausibility, but he could have cut the occasional repeat. I mean, some of us have a train to catch.'

I didn't believe the half of it, but it had been a long time since my last discussion about classical music in English, and I didn't want it fizzling out early just because we agreed with each other.

'I must say *Alcina* seems very naturalistic to me.'

'Professor, that is the last adjective one could use.'

'But *my dear fellow*,' he said, without sounding in the least patronising, yet inflecting his voice in obvious readiness for a coup de grâce, 'isn't that what *you* are doing here?'

'I beg your pardon?'

'Haven't you exiled yourself to what some would call "the middle of nowhere" in order to consider your feelings ad nauseam, and with many repetitions? You may find that there are people out there waiting for your internal aria to end, so that you can get on with things.'

His tone was compassionate, which only made the ensuing pause more awkward. Booker made an earnest examination of the label on the wine bottle. The Professor had not finished making his point.

'What do you think you've resolved here that you couldn't have gleaned in a single night with Handel?'

Served me right, really. I was in no position to lambast Handel's leisurely way with a plot when all the evidence proved I had lost my own. For a moment I considered reprising the swing analogy, but since we had discovered that nobody knew what swing was until they heard it, the sum total of my intended personal revelations thus far was less than zero. I had had this notion that when life's dissatisfactions mounted up, you should stop everything, go away somewhere nice and figure it out. This now appeared to be as useful a tactic as another one of Alcina's *da capos* after three hours of singing. Even this was a bad analogy; Handel would have been a big help, actually.

Booker leaned forward and smiled. 'The Professor has a point. To quote a certain person of my acquaintance . . . *you should get out more.*'

The irony of such advice being dispensed in the south of France was not lost on me. I smiled back at Booker and the Professor.

'That sounds like the cue for a song,' I said.

'And I have just the song for you tonight,' Booker replied. 'Let's go back to the shed, where all will be revealed. We'll bail up Pete en route; I might even see if the Swedes are at home. *Allez-y!*'

What had begun as a session of jazz therapy turned into a small party. Pete, by now in his civvies, was easily coaxed away from his kitchen easel and back to what Booker called the House of Angora. Windows, bottles and a piano lid were opened and Booker exercised his stride muscles with James P. Johnson's *The Mule Walk*. The Swedes' concern for their 'uncle' next door had blossomed into a friendship after all, for they came straight to the shed door at the first *plonks* from his pumping left hand. With seven of us standing around the piano, the tiny place was full to bursting. Some of the girls looked at Booker – glasses perched on the end of his nose, hands moving about the keyboard in a surprisingly gentle way, considering all the notes that were created – as if he were an exotic species of insect. Stride was new to them. Twenty-two year old Swedes didn't get much of this in their usual Stockholm nightspots.

'Take a break, old bean,' I suggested. 'What about that song you promised me?'

'I have it here on CD,' he said. 'Cleaning up the original took a lot of work. Someone had been using it as a dinner plate after playing the sides with a knitting needle. But the effort was worth it, I think.'

An extended introduction featured a rhythm section of strumming banjo and the *oom-pah* of a tuba. This was not New Orleans jazz, but popular dance music.

'It's half over, and nobody's sung yet,' I observed.

'Patience,' Booker counselled. 'It's the standard format of the time. There's nothing great about the song; just a good product from the music factory that was Tin Pan Alley. The guy who wrote the words, Charles Tobias, was a vaudevillian who ended up running his own publishing firm in the mid-20s. Here we go.'

A trio of male voices came in, singing close harmony. You could almost smell the hair oil.

When you're all alone, any old night
And you're feeling out of tune
Pick up your hat, close up your flat
Get out, get under the moon!

'Cute,' I commented.

'And popular,' chimed Booker. 'Lots of artists rushed to cover this one when it came out in 1928. Helen Kane was one of them. She was the original 'Boop-Boop-A-Doop' Girl whose singing style was copied by the cartoon Betty Boop and parodied much later by Marilyn Monroe. A very young Bing Crosby also recorded a version. This is a good dance band of the time, the Hal Kemp Orchestra. Notice how the tuba actually keeps the rhythm buoyant, rather than pinning the whole thing down. It isn't easy.'

Look! Look! Look at the stars above
Look, look, look at those sweeties love
Oh, boy, give me a night in June!

'It ain't Handel,' I pronounced during the playout, recalling my earlier conversation with the Professor.

'True, but it's all very well being told that music is superior because it allegedly presents us with some fundamental truth,' said Booker. 'This isn't always helpful, because that "truth" is only what you *think* it is. Sometimes, as in a lyric like this, it's far more useful to get a bit of plain *advice*, don't you think?'

'Get out and get under the moon,' I mused. 'It's not a bad tip.'

'Hey guys!' Pete exclaimed, raising his head above the huddle of blondes. 'I've just been telling the girls about my Zorro exploits up at the castle, and they wanna go up there now to have a look! Are you comin' too?'

Darkness had fallen and much red wine consumed during and after dinner, but Booker and I exchanged glances and shrugged. 'If the idea's good enough for Bing Crosby, it's good enough for me,' I said.

Our intrepid band walked uphill and out of the village, the conversation sounding unnaturally loud in the silence. On the way, I paused outside the orgasm window, but the couple inside were keeping their peace tonight. Within minutes the eerie form of fourteenth-century Roquevaire reared up over us, its crumbling turrets limned by the moon. Although Pete had brought a torch, it would not be needed. With precise, practised movement, he began to bound up a ramp of rubble leading to a ledge running along a high wall.

'*Whoa!*' we cried out, moving unsteadily behind him. I

suspected our balance problems were not entirely due to the shifting stones under our feet. We joined hands with the Swedes – one of the nicer consequences of climbing by moonlight – and inched in a Scandanavian daisy chain onto the ledge. I brought up the rear.

'Come along to the end here,' called out Pete. He was standing near an indentation in the wall that interrupted the ledge's course. 'And don't look down.'

Hearing this instruction, I looked down. With our backs to the moon, and the shadow cast by the wall, it was impossible to make out anything in the darkness beneath our feet. 'Pete, how high up *are* we?' I yelled, trying to sound insouciant.

'About forty feet, I guess.'

'*Ow*,' cried out Inge ahead of me as I involuntarily dug a finger into the underside of her wrist. Just be glad I'm a nail biter, I thought, between two waves of mild panic. The rest of the group whistled with excitement. How pissed *were* they?

Pete pivoted on his feet and leapt into the darkness, landing neatly where the ledge resumed. 'There's just a step here over this gap,' he explained helpfully. Booker had arrived at the spot and was priming himself for the jump. He had done this before.

That's no bloody *step*, I thought again, as the waves of panic began to develop foaming crests that blotted out the stars. One by one, the white forms of the Swedes slipped easily through the ether and materialised on the far side of the chasm. Inge broke free of my grasp and joined them.

'Okay – now it's your turn!' Pete said excitedly, as if he were telling me that I had won the car. 'Just don't look down.' The others were already continuing their progress along the ledge. Clearly, for them this had been no big deal.

I looked down. The world was black and spinning like a 78 record. How pissed was *I*?

'*Nah*, Pete. I think I might just double back and wait for you all at the shed.'

'C'mon – it's nothing much more than a big step.'

The wave crests broke, thundering down onto my head. 'Honestly, Pete – I don't think I can do this.'

At that moment, and of all the things in the world, the sound of a fiddle floated up from the village below. Our mysterious player was on his balcony, pouring his reassuring moonlight lilt into the soft night wind.

'*Amigo! Jump!*' commanded Pete. 'You can do this! Just . . . *be Zorro!*'

Two hours earlier I had been talking about the implausibility of opera, and now I was about to die like bloody Tosca, falling off a castle. Well, you wanted your midlife adventure, I reminded myself, and now you're getting it: pretending to be a fictional Mexican outlaw and leaping across parapets under the moon while someone serenades you on the violin. I raised my eyes to look straight ahead, took a deep breath, and flung myself into the path of the rising melody. Immediately I felt a steadying grip on my elbow as my feet touched stone. When I looked back, I saw the 'leap' had been less than four feet.

Only Pete's eyes and teeth were visible in the silhouette of his face. For an instant, he looked just like his hero.

'See, *amigo*?' he said. 'Sometimes, you just gotta *jump*.'

EIGHT

CARAVAN

ISAVOURED THAT LEAP for weeks. It taught me something I could not have learned from a Handel opera, something to throw back nonchalantly at the Professor the next time we discussed music and metaphysics in a wine bar.

It was unlikely that a return bout would take place at the same venue in the short term, however. Not that the topic was exhausted, but the wine bar was closed. There had been a contretemps with the police when they attended the scene late one night in response to complaints about the noise. Detail was sketchy. One story had it that the owner responded to an official request to 'keep it down' by throwing a perfectly good glass of red wine over the gendarme's uniform. A scuffle ensued, and a notice of contravention was posted on the bar's locked doors the next day.

Booker was delighted. 'The crowd there was too unsavoury,' he explained. 'One night I was playing *Carolina Shout* on their piano when a drunk stumbled over, demanded to hear *House Of The Rising Sun*, and brought up his dinner. I couldn't decide which was more offensive: the vomiting, or the choice of song.'

Meanwhile, the *Joli Jeu* had problems of its own. The sudden loss of Ivan had left the bass section in tatters. The Artist could not manage alone, so the Maestro moved Pete down a part and transferred several altos to help me on the tenor line. Not only did we now sound as if we were all on helium, but Pete's vocal attempts on low notes during the Tchaikovsky, redolent of a prolonged belch, were more Tibetan than Russian. The upside of this was that our director now raised her arms higher on the upbeat, having taken heed of my technical tips delivered during our post-rehearsal wine consultations.

Only Nini seemed relaxed as we drew closer to the day of the concert. 'Gary has left town,' she informed me. 'The property sale did not happen.'

My French was improving. 'And what is not so good with Gary?' I said.

'The money never came from LA. He did not *have* any money.'

I felt sorry for Gary, and for us. He had gone back to Los Angeles, when we could have used him in the bass section.

In the end, the concert did not go too badly. The Artist's voice packed up early, so he was sent off after our second madrigal to help out with serving the interval drinks. Anticipating such a turn of events, our *chef* imported some male reinforcements from a choir in Alès for the day on an errand of mercy. One of the new tenors looked as outdoorsy as she did. Worse, I noted how her upbeat was particularly emphatic when she faced him – the hussy.

Afterwards, the choir celebrated at the Commerce across the square. All the applause was good for our morale. Plans were discussed to consolidate our forces for the next performance in the autumn. The *chef* sat at the next table, making a considerable (and what I would have said to be over-enthusiastic, had anyone cared to ask me) effort to cajole the men from Alès into staying on. The outdoorsy tenor looked interested. I sensed that our conducting tutorials were at an end. Which was just as well, because so too was my time in the village.

'Oh, *non!*' exclaimed some of the sopranos, the two words rhyming, when I made my announcement over a second round of beers. At least *they* knew a good tenor when they had one. I reassured them that they were not being deserted for some clandestine rival group in cahoots with the disappearing Roger and the elusive Ivan; it was simply time to move on. My two months in the village were up. Aline's brother was slated as the next tenant in the basement, and he was due any day.

Despite having deep thoughts on quiet evenings as I

cooked pasta to the sounds of the flowing Vidourle and its ducks, I had not received any *Walden*esque epiphanies, consoling myself that Thoreau had to stick it out in his cabin by a pond for two years. Nor had I heard anything that might translate into a hit song à la *Frenesi* and Artie Shaw. The *Tchaikovsky Tibetan Rap* didn't have quite the same ring to it, though it will doubtless be attempted sooner or later.

My singing colleagues, the expatriate colony of record collectors and the rest of the townspeople who sat gossiping in the bars or around the fountain would have been incredulous if I had suggested that just hanging out with them was going to give me some clues on how to lead a richer, fuller life. 'You came all that way just to be *here*?' was the subtext I detected in early conversations, when I described exchanging a sunny city of long coastal beaches for the seclusion of a basement.

They had a point. They were not doing anything special when it came to the technique of living. Nor did adventure, romance or revelation confine themselves to a few picturesque locales. Castles might be rare in your or my part of the world, but a moon to be got under is everywhere.

While intense self-absorption – the main psychic affliction of men over forty – had not added anything to my mental pocketbook of home-hewn philosophy, the action of just *doing* things had proved far more instructive. And, in retrospect, I had not been doing enough. It is a pitifully static sojourn indeed when the highlight turns out to have been a four-foot jump. I had to be careful; all thought and no action could turn one into a very dull middle-aged boy. Just think how much more exciting *Walden* would have been with even a single car chase.

Luckily, my adventure was not yet over. The phrase 'as chance would have it' is such a flimsy segue, but I chose not to quibble about serendipity when friends asked me if I could move on to look after their lonely and neglected old farmhouse on the other side of the Rhône, starting as soon as I liked and continuing through the rest of the year. The *maison secondaire* was located in the Lubéron, lately the official face of Provence in best-selling travel books, despite the region's long continuation further east to the Italian border. Apart from Tuscany, it is hard to think of another place on earth that is more mythologised at present.

For some in the village, I may as well have been travelling to another planet. 'But you are going away to Provence!' they said in surprise. 'We will never see you.' Although the next planet was about 120 kilometres away, the rural French do not roam far from their patch. Not long ago, I was talking with a retired headmistress who lived in a hamlet near Cluny, in Burgundy. It is perhaps three hours by car from Paris, from where – as I explained to her – I had just come.

'Ah, *Paris*,' she murmured with the wonder of an

astronomer contemplating a distant star. '*Oui*, I was there once.'

'When?' I was surprised she had made only one visit.

'I think it was 1932.'

The southerners are even less curious. During a dinner just outside the city of Pau with a woman in her sixties, I mentioned an expedition the next morning that would take me through the Pyrénées and into Spain. Would the weather change much immediately beyond the mountains? I asked. She didn't know, she replied. She had never been to Spain. The border was forty kilometres away from where we sat.

Leaving the village was as inconsequential an event as my arrival. The Crumbs were out when I dropped off the key – Aline taking a gym class, Robert on his regular constitutional in the Mer equipped with pen and paper – and Pete was away from his kitchen, probably up a wall or a castle somewhere. The Professor had left for his apartment in Lucca, forsaking Handel for the birthplace of Puccini. Standing under the Artist's plaque and knocking fruitlessly on his door, I heard once more the fiddler opposite whose nocturnal bowings had levitated me around Roquevaire last full moon.

The vista of rooftops below reminded me of my reverie about Maxine Sullivan, two months, six choir rehearsals and a jump ago. At least, I thought it was two months ago. Time tends to lose its way among these old houses until chased out of cul-de-sacs by the tolling of a bell, or the first tray of filled wine glasses. Away from the village, up in the Mer where Crumb would be sketching under a shrub, time vanishes altogether; one considers only that one is alive. Without time's drumbeat, being alive and old is the same as being alive and young, so to worry about being positioned somewhere in between is irrelevant. Up among those ancient castle ruins and primeval stones, the span of a life makes no difference.

As I walked back down the incline to the House of Angora, the multicoloured cyclist veered out from her side street. This time she stopped in front of me and held out her hand. '*Au revoir, monsieur*,' she said.

These spare courtesies – the *bonjours*, this farewell – were the only words we ever exchanged. To barely know someone, and be content to leave it at that, can be one of the most delicate of pleasures.

A trombone was playing a sinuous and familiar tune over jungle drums upstairs in the goat shed. Booker was in.

'Just in time to hear Juan Tizol in his prime. He was one of Duke Ellington's best players, and they collaborated in writing *Caravan* in 1937. I've just given it the Treatment for a French release. The tune became an unfortunate staple of certain gentlemen's establishments . . .'

'You mean strip clubs.'

'Ironic, isn't it, that the ultimate striptease anthem was penned by a Duke? Still, once you disregard its subsequent abuses and go back to the original you find a masterpiece of orchestration. I mean, that opening, with tom-toms, Burmese gong, a Chinese cymbal.' His voice took on a 1940s newsreel commentator's stridency. 'Escape! Exotic locations! Arcane rituals! *You are there.*'

'Well, my own caravan is about to pull out of town, heading for exotic locations further east. I've hired a Peugeot.'

'Excellent. Give our regards to all the rich people. And don't forget to send a postcard.'

It was Nini who came to wave goodbye, handing me a deluxe *spéciale* as a way of winding down after the long (two-hour) journey. As I crossed the Pont Vieux, a light rain began to fall, and the receding face of the village turned grey and flat, looking just as it had when I first saw it two months before. Perhaps I *was* going to another planet, after all.

There was one more call to make before heading for the Rhône. I cut due north across the ancient river plain to arrive at Cardet and the Farrells'. Meg and Micheal had just returned from Montpellier and a slew of doctors' appointments about his condition.

Micheal proposed that he and I go to the local bar with such quiet urgency in his voice that I couldn't refuse, even though I had the afternoon drive ahead of me. It was the same bar in which he had first enquired about places for sale twelve years before. Photographs of the local rugby teams lined the walls. The huge alsatian sat near the front door, eyeing a table at which six burly locals prepared to tuck into their roast pigeons and jellied pigs' feet. Everyone in the bar wished them a *bon appétit*.

It was a silly question, but I sensed that Micheal wanted the prompt. 'How was Montpellier?'

'No fuckin' good. The chemo hasn't worked, and the cancer's back on the move. I'm gonna need a big operation. They'll take out more of my fuckin' jaw and I'll be in hospital for a while. It's not good. I'm fuckin' worried about it.'

He looked it, too. Who could blame him? Years of fending off this vicious yapping dog dancing around him, and now the little bastard was coming back for another bite. The expression in his eyes reduced all of my midlife meditations to the level of puerility. Even my recent conclusions about time had been made under the arrogant presumption that I would always have more of it. This is more than anyone can expect.

'Well, you've come this far, Micheal. Once the doctors have whipped it out again you can get on with things, just like all those times before.' So came the platitudes, all given dutifully.

But he continued to look out through the window and watch time passing quickly in the street.

I never saw the Vaucluse before it became famous, and cannot tell you how much things have changed since it was given a starring role in certain books. Looked at through a car window, it does exude the sleek glamour of celebrity, even if, like certain A-list stars, it is famous of its own accord without actually doing anything. It is the Elizabeth Taylor of *départements*: plush, lazy and ravished repeatedly by wealthy men.

You notice the difference as soon as you cross the Rhône and loop around the bottom of Avignon, heading west on the Cavaillon road. Things become more verdant. Plants are keener to put down roots here than in the often scrubby Gard, and they are better dressed, with superior posture, all those cypresses with their straight spines and noses in the air. Shortly after this, the Lubéron mountains heave up on the left and escort you for the rest of the drive, like very, very large department store doormen pointing the way to the luxury furniture. And if you don't have the money, you don't go in.

My destination was Ansouis, a village much smaller than

the one I had left. Turning off the main road between Cavaillon and Pertuis, you follow a narrow one that seems to have no idea where it is going. Suddenly, a thirteenth-century château on the crown of a hill sails into view, tacking majestically across the valley under the wind power of a single tall flag placed amidships as you turn the steering wheel of your car back and forth. This is Ansouis' beacon, a stately pile in which the same family have lived for more than seven hundred years, avoiding even those moments in the French Revolution most inimical to the lives of aristocrats, and thereby saving themselves the bother of ever having to have their mail redirected. The modest village spilling down the hill from the base of the château's walls is relaxed enough to sacrifice a fine northerly view of the Lubéron in favour of the gentler (and sunnier) southern slope.

By now I knew how a village worked from the ground up – to be more precise, from the *under*ground up – after two months of living closer to the centre of the earth than 1,800 fellow dwellers. I would put this new expertise to work tomorrow. For now, Ansouis scudded by as I literally headed for the hills, on one of which my friends' property promised a more elevated aspect than a basement could provide. A minute later I left the sealed road, drove through a field of vines and climbed a steeply graded zigzag. A final sharp swerve and the car stopped at an old farmhouse, bent in a U-shape around a courtyard. I turned down Duke Ellington on the car CD player, blinked, and whispered to myself.

'Shit a brick.'

It is very disconcerting to see a definitive example of something you have only read about in books and imagined. The 'sleepy Provençal farmhouse' ranks high as a dream experience in the popular imagination. Well, this was it. I half expected my outstretched hand to pass through the textured stone walls as if they were smoke, or that the outlook of lavender, vines, and in-ground swimming pool surrounded by olive trees, all on successively higher terraces nestled into a forested hillside with no other houses in sight, would shimmer before my eyes like a mirage and turn back into a suburban petrol station. But everything was stable and rock solid as I stepped inside the house to a welcoming coolness. From an upstairs bathroom I could look back at the château of Ansouis, now lying securely at anchor in the middle of the plain.

There was a new challenge for me in living like this. What would be blissful privacy on sunny days might become gnawing isolation when the rain and cold winds came to call later in the year. Despite Thoreau's assertion that solitude was just a state of mind, I could see that living alone up on a hill would be a more hermetic experience than living alone inside a village, where socialising commenced at the front door. I was going to have to chase people if I wanted to talk to them;

not a good look in the country. But I wouldn't kid myself. This was still *Walden* meets *Dynasty*.

One thing I have never really liked about memoirs set in the south of France is their inevitable moments of congratulatory self-indulgence. If you feel the same way, you will perhaps turn the page quickly before I divulge that on my first evening I poured out a glass of cool white wine, walked past the lavender and vines, reclined on grass with one foot dipped in the pool, breathed warm, clear air while watching points of light flicker to life in the valley and the sky, and reflected on my good fortune.

At least I have kept it brief.

NINE

TIME ON MY HANDS

GEORGE SHEARING (PIANO), LONDON, 1942

'*UN GRAND CRÈME, s'il vous plaît, Gérard.*'
'*Un crème!* Okay, Mister Chris.'

Each morning I made a fifteen-minute walk from the quiet of the farmhouse to the quiet of the village. Following the line of sight to the fluttering flag atop the château, I would proceed down my zigzag of unsealed road, through yet more vines, and up to the *place* des Hôtes and the Ansouis hot spot, the Bar des Sports.

I suppose you have to call a bar something, if only to give directions to strangers. And in time it would prove to be more convenient to suggest to visitors or couriers that we rendezvous at the Bar des Sports in lieu of the farmhouse, which was too difficult for strangers to find. But having a name on your bar matters little when it is the only one in town, and Ansouis is a place that is only big enough to sustain one of anything.

Anyway, the title was a misnomer. There were no sporting memorabilia on the walls, like the rugby shrine in Cardet; nor did the radio behind the bar ever blare out football commentary, relying instead on slow classic hits of the 80s like *Don't Give Up* or *Wonderful Life*. The other patrons downing an early *pastis* before ten in the morning were not about to represent France in any international sporting event. It was left to the barman, Gérard, to live up to the advertising by wearing a football jersey every day, something he did with genuine commitment, being a native of Marseilles and a former player, though a short one.

Summer was beginning to bear down on the place, and the climbing temperatures dictated the order of my breakfast procession. First stop, the village's sole *boulangerie* where Corinne, the baker's wife, would have an almond croissant bagged and ready to go. 'What will you be doing today?' she asked me every time, and I do not think I ever gave her a satisfactory answer. 'We'll see when the time comes,' was the best I could do.

The next port of call was the village's *agence de presse*. Bruno, the ruddy proprietor, would shake my hand and talk about the weather in an impenetrable Provençal accent. That was what I supposed to be the subject, anyway. His heartiness was infectious, and I would nod and say '*oui, chaud*' to everything he rattled out at such speed. I figured that whether it was the weather, his marriage, or village gossip, the content was bound to be hot.

Finally, I entered the Bar des Sports to bid a good morning

to everyone present, and perform a de rigueur handshake with Gérard, followed by our brief colloquy. My stock request for *un crème* had little to do with the business of ordering a white coffee, and everything to do with the building of rapport; learning to read each other's mood that day through the subtle variations in our tone. A clipped delivery from me would mean that the water pump at the farmhouse was dying, and I had been reduced to showering under a dripping tap. A bright response from Gérard meant he was due to pick up his young son from his ex-wife and take him to a football match. Ask a friend how they are feeling, and their answer will often mask the truth; but have a stranger request a cup of coffee twenty times, and you will know their soul.

After baring my soul at the bar, I would take a seat under one of the trees in the square and watch the world go by. Most days, it didn't. The world was out there going someplace else. It could have been looking for a restaurant, which was more than Ansouis could provide. There had been a restaurant at some point, with a slightly surreal name like *L'Olive Bleue*, but it closed. Perhaps nobody understood why an olive should be blue, or there weren't enough people in Ansouis to keep it afloat, or the world couldn't find it.

There was also stiff daytime competition from the Bar des Sports. On weekends a small barbeque was trundled out into the street, and a lunch of *andouillettes* with chips and salad served to an adoring clientele. (*Andouillettes* are what remain of a pig after you have thrown its carcass into the Café du Commerce.) This al fresco feast was prepared under the watchful eye of Roberte, the forty-something owner, who had been left with the bar when her husband died prematurely of a heart attack, pushed over the edge by that last ill-advised *andouillette*.

Like many teenage brides released from marital servitude in their prime, Roberte was said to have blossomed in widowhood. She now wore slinky tops and was squired by one of the château's gardeners. I thought Roberte would be quite a catch in these parts. As the village's only businesswoman, she was by default the most successful. A blue olive didn't stand a chance.

After about a month of regular visits to the bar, something momentous happened one morning that confirmed the elevation of my status beyond that of a mere tourist. Instead of responding to my *bonjour* with one of her own and a bemused smile (itself a step up from the polite blankness accorded to strangers), Roberte stepped out from behind the bar, walked over to me with her stiff-legged gait, leaned forward, and positioned her face for the double-cheeker. I tell you: the earth moved.

'Wow! You don't get a welcome like that in Paris,' I said, cementing our solidarity.

'Yes, that's Paris,' she agreed disdainfully. 'I went there once.'

'When was this?' I was no longer surprised that the

750-kilometre trip to her country's capital was thought to be worth doing only once in a southerner's lifetime.

'I think it was 1973.'

As a newly appointed honorary villager, the least I could do was say the name of the place like a local. 'Onn-SWEES,' Roberte insisted, with a hard final 's' that northerners normally leave out. This pronunciation confused French passers-by from other regions who, when stopping to ask where they were, would scratch their heads at the reply and wonder how they ended up in Switzerland.

That same morning of the small earthquake I was sitting in the *place*, touching my hand to my cheeks where Roberte had been and rejoicing in my temporary citizenship (conferred without having to join a choir), when a great hairy hand landed on my copy of the *International Herald Tribune*.

'G'day,' the hand's owner said. 'What's the news?'

An unmistakably Australian voice boomed out of an unmistakably Mediterranean hairless head that shone like a nearby planet in the sun's glare. Hearing an accent like my own for the first time in months was an appropriate after-shock of that morning's suspension of formalities at the bar. Today, no one would be a stranger. We launched into an immediate exchange of life histories.

Matt was a big – but by no means the biggest – son of Lebanese immigrants who became such successful business people in their adopted country that the boys were able to spend their adolescence bulking up in Sydney beachside affluence.

Matt was now a winemaker. This was his fifth tour of duty in Provence, making the so-called New World style of wine for an English company to sell into British supermarkets.

'What is this New World style?' I asked.

'New World wines have an obvious and consistent flavour: clean, crisp, fruit-driven, in your face. It's what the market wants across the Channel. It's what the market seems to want everywhere, except in France. The French have got the shits because it's killing export sales of their *appellation d'origine controlée* stuff. Their Old World wines are always idiosyncratic, but that's too unreliable for the mass market. People want to know what they're getting, and if they like it, they want it to taste the same the next time they pull it off a supermarket shelf.'

'So the English slip an Australian into Old World heartland to make a particular style of wine because you know how to do it . . .'

'. . . and the French don't. Or at least, it's not the way they choose to do it. As far as the old AOC types are concerned, I'm the enemy. But the guys at the co-op here are fine about it. They give me a couple of vats and let me do my own thing with the grapes that come in.'

He loved it, too. A bit of cutlass work on the landlubbers down at the local winery wouldn't have raised a patina of sweat on that shiny head. With his striped T-shirt, single earring and blustering voice, Matt looked like a pirate on shore leave.

On my return from the village I found a wooden table in the farmhouse courtyard. A hand-written note lying on top welcomed me to the Lubéron and asked if I would like to come for dinner. The table here is now repaired, it concluded. It was signed *Alain, ébéniste.*

It was kind of a tradesman to extend such an invitation to a stranger who wasn't even a client, but I had been forewarned about such regional hospitality by various travel memoirs. These gorgeous little Lubéron people, I thought, thrilled to the marrow.

I rang Alain in a grateful twitter. 'This is such a very . . . *Provençal* thing to do. Thank you.'

'It is no problem,' he assured me in a calm voice. 'We look forward to seeing you on Thursday. By the way – I come from Paris.'

The village of Bastide des Jourdans lies about half an hour's drive further east from Ansouis over gentle swells of vine-covered hills. As arranged, Alain was waiting for me outside the only bar in town, a gentle, professorial figure who would have looked as completely at home in Oxford marking up a thesis as he felt when cutting the precise angle of the join on a benchtop.

Alain's home was one of those places with so many stairways and corridors burrowing in all directions that I eventually gave up any hope of finding my way out. A horde of children spilled in and out of rooms, allowing pop music to blare through open doors. Our tour ended in a large kitchen and dining room with a window opening out to the street, its sill about six feet above the pavement.

Regional French dining culture still dictates that the family eats together at table. This is fine, as long as there is just one family involved. But to be middle-aged today can often mean being midway through a succession of families, just as a modern working life can incorporate a succession of careers. When interested parties from yesterday and today are all present and accounted for, this requires a very large table indeed; and so it was here. Alain and his wife Françoise had both been married before, and their extended families were assembled to meet an exotic Antipodean who promised to be an endless source of spoken French malapropisms.

Therefore, it was a roomful of people who rose to meet me. They included Alain's sister and brother-in-law, Françoise's brother and sister-in-law, Alain's children from his first marriage, one of Françoise's children from *her* first marriage, various nieces and nephews, and some other kids I couldn't place. A number of cats regarded us from their positions on nearby cabinets. Leading this extensive cast was *maman*, Françoise's mother, who was initially all smiles, but became more taciturn as the meal progressed.

Françoise was a charmer, cooing and shimmering *à table* as she ladled *soupe au pistou* from a large pot (vegetables and pasta in a bouillon, served with lashings of gruyère, parmesan and fresh pesto). It was almost inconceivable that she might have to prepare food on this scale every night. Later, she confided to me that she suffered from sciatica. Observing the size of her soup pot, I wasn't surprised.

It was a boisterous table, mainly because I talked animatedly about myself, making what I thought to be whimsical and amusing observations about being so adventurous in France at my time of life. Everyone nodded and laughed in not quite the right places of the narrative. My flow was halted briefly when a young boy (who may or may not have been related to anybody) tapped the arm of the adult next to him to ask what it was that I was saying. Now and then a neighbour's head appeared in the window, severed Godot-like by the line of the sill, to call over to Françoise while nodding at me, 'Is he still going?'

One of the brothers-in-law was a clarinettist who shared my professed admiration for Artie Shaw and Benny Goodman.

People didn't play music with the same feeling any more, he theorised, before turning his wrath on the modern-day French conductor Pierre Boulez, whom he thought a cold fish. There was no disagreement from the rest of the table. I doubted they had heard of Pierre Boulez.

Suddenly *maman* piped up from her place at the end of the table, where she had been sitting mute for the better part of an hour.

'They're getting very big, aren't they?'

An awkward pause. I was not sure if *maman* was commenting on my choice of words. Françoise was bold enough to demand clarification.

'What did you say, *maman*?'

'I said, they're *getting very big*,' insisted the old lady. 'They weren't as big last year.' She turned briefly to me. 'What do *you* think?'

A dozen pairs of eyes swivelled in my direction, and then followed *maman*'s gaze to Alain's eldest daughter Amélie, who had just returned to the table after freshening her make-up in the serious manner peculiar to fifteen year olds. Finally, the euro dropped for all of us. *Maman* was commenting on Amélie's breasts.

'*Maman*, I'm sure that our guest doesn't think anything,' protested Françoise.

There was a further pause. I was expected to make some

comment in response to *maman*, obviously. Glancing down the table at Amélie, I was ready to concede that, in all fairness, *maman* had a valid point. Instead, I offered some bread to the brother-in-law.

'Don't you think Boulez is good when he conducts Debussy?' I asked, trying to bring the topic back to something about which the table would have no opinion. *Maman* was not deterred.

'Last year they were just right. Now there's too much of them.'

'Really, *maman!*' remonstrated Françoise. 'Amélie is just growing up! Last year she was only fourteen. This is what happens when you are fifteen.'

'Well, it didn't happen to me. If she keeps going like this, she'll have problems when she is eighteen.'

'I think Boulez has an unequalled ear for orchestral balance,' I opined to the clarinettist, who paid me no attention.

'That dress doesn't help,' *maman* continued. 'There's practically no material there to keep anything in. One of them is almost in her soup.'

'*Maman*, I think Amélie looks very pretty in her little summer ensemble,' said a sister – or was it a sister-in-law? – leaping into the fray. 'And I'm sure that she doesn't like to be spoken about like this . . . do you, *chérie*?'

Amélie smiled knowingly. 'Oh, I don't mind,' she said.

'Did you know that Boulez was an Egyptian princess in a former life?' I threw at anybody. But it was too late. Boulez and I had been swept aside by a family matter of more immediate concern. The increasingly self-aware Amélie was dominating the table by her very presence, as I suspected would be the case for the next few summers. Such is life, I reflected. The wisdom of middle age is passed over by a concern for appearances; brains trounced by boobs. I began to understand the weight-stripping anxiety of your typical middle-aged female television weather presenter.

Things settled down when Amélie left the table to adjust her dress. I picked up my thread of conversation, but the momentum was gone. Still, I pushed on, as one must do in midlife – with attempted grace, but upstaged nevertheless.

Driving back to the farmhouse that evening, the CD compilation of shellac highlights that Booker had made for me as a parting gift reached a track called *Time On My Hands*, recorded in 1942 by the young pianist George Shearing. The tune is by Vincent Youmans, who made his career in the 20s, capturing the time's quintessential glitter with his musical *No, No, Nanette*. Both his and the decade's glitter ran out at about the same time. *Time On My Hands* came from a 1930 musical flop called *Smiles* that failed to elicit any of the same from grim-faced Broadway audiences, running for only sixty-three performances, despite the lure of Fred and Adele Astaire in the cast. To compound the irony, time on *his* hands was something that Youmans did not have. He was diagnosed with tuberculosis in his thirties and spent much of the remainder of his life in sanatoriums, going bankrupt along the way. The disease killed him in 1946, when he was just forty-seven.

It is one of those Youmans tunes that start as more an oscillation than a melody (rather like *Tea For Two* and *I Want To Be Happy*, both from *No, No, Nanette*), curiously at odds with the expansiveness implied by the song's title. Maybe Youmans was hinting that it wasn't a good thing. Was having time on your hands really so desirable? It is *such* a slippery currency; measurable, but formless, inherently valueless and liable to run out unless spent.

No one I had met here in the Lubéron – except me, perhaps – was letting time slip through his or her fingers. Everybody of my vintage or older was making fresh starts for the second or third time, which was just as well, because the place was too expensive for anybody to start from scratch.

My favourite example was an American woman who came to live in Provence with her fourth husband, imagining that a complete change of scene might help their marriage survive. He promptly ran off with another woman to live in Avignon, leaving his wife alone, unemployed, and on the high side of fifty – but with no inclination to go scuttling home across the Atlantic. A local real estate agent thought her native English and experience as a New York-based psychotherapist might be helpful in selling property to the increasingly large numbers of British and Americans who were combing the area. He offered her a desk, a telephone and a commission.

Her timing, at the beginning of the Provence boom, was impeccable. Twenty years later, the errant husband had died, and she was a partner in one of the most successful property agencies in the Vaucluse, specialising in the top end of the market. Her clients ranged from music publishing moguls to at least one Hollywood film star, and they adored her for her brusque candour. One happy customer made her the god-mother to his next child. She had sold the farmhouse outside Ansouis to my friends.

Moreover, she decided that four marriages were enough.

'Oh *Gaad*, are you kidding? I couldn't go through that again,' she said as we lunched at one of her regular places in the village of Goult, on the north side of the Lubéron. Four-wheel-drive landcruisers rumbled up and down the narrow street in front of us, driven by foreign investors looking for something else to buy – perhaps from her. 'At my age, you don't need any more of that hoo-hah. I'm much happier sharing my house with Chekhov, the cat.'

'I'm surprised that by marriage number four you couldn't see the white water ahead. Especially since you were a psychotherapist. What did he do?'

'He was a psychotherapist as well.'

This news confounded much of my adventure's purpose. What use was there in trying to make sense of the rest of your life at my age, when it could all still go pear-shaped? One could not even rely on probabilities. If two smart professionals in their middle years could not end up with better-than-even odds on the outcome of a marriage – one entered into with the benefit of life experience, self-knowledge, and the noble scars from previous attempts – then what hope was there for the rest of us? And not just marriage, over which we can presume to exercise an element of control, but in other issues where chance or the tide of circumstance – in a word, *fate* – rushes in from the wings and pulls our pants down?

I was back where I had been in the Gard, stranded in my conversation with the Professor in a wine bar, with nothing more to offer in response to his enquiry about the lessons learned from protracted self-reflection than a question mark. Maybe I should polish up this question mark, this dubious trophy, and hang it somewhere in my mind. Choosing the question in preference to the answer, embracing uncertainty:

what else is adventure for? Even a four-foot jump can go wrong. People can live in beautiful places and still get ill. A country drive can be wrecked by a passing pig. Symphonies can change key by the end. There's always the chance of rain.

By early September the vines looked as if they had come home dishevelled after a night on the tiles. After a hot August, and the increasing burden of carrying their ripening fruit, they looked ready to lose their fancy clothes and have a rest. The *vendange* was imminent, and people like Matt would soon swing into action.

I had visited friends in Burgundy and was driving down the major north–south highway, the Route du Soleil, when the sky blackened in the middle of the afternoon and it began to rain so violently that traffic slowed to a halt. No windscreen wiper could prevail against such a downpour. Just as suddenly as it had begun, the tempest moved on, and I nursed the car forward slowly through several inches of water. The Sunshine Road had turned into a shallow river in minutes.

Before I turned left into Provence, I looked in the direction of the Gard. A huge black cloud sat right over it, dropping thick curtains of rain that completely obscured the distant line of the Cévennes. They were having a right old bucketing over there, I reckoned. The Vaucluse to my left looked clearer. I hoped the farmhouse was secure.

The sky reclaimed a disingenuous brightness (who, *me*? it said) as I passed Ansouis, but there was still plenty of evidence of its recent tantrum once I turned off the sealed road. A thick brown slush blanketed the field at the foot of the hill, and there were the beginnings of two large damp patches in my bedroom ceiling from undetected gaps in the roof. This was no disaster; the tiles were loose-laid and could be hauled back into position, and there were still enough warm days left of summer to dry everything out. Nothing had been damaged that couldn't be fixed, and now the Peugeot was spotlessly clean after the carwash-strength downpour. Quite a relief, really.

But the lady television weather presenter without a body didn't look too pleased about things the next day. The video footage accompanying her report made surreal viewing, confirming that what I had seen over the Gard was a disaster. These were the heaviest rains the *département* had ever recorded, totalling in one day as much as Paris receives in a year. Eighty-five percent of the area was under water. Sommiéres looked like Venice, cars drifting through its streets like gondolas. It looked as if twenty-four people had lost their lives.

I tried to ring my friends on the other side of the Rhône, but telephone lines were down. Another day passed, and the magnitude of the catastrophe became more apparent. People were being airlifted from the roofs of their houses, and entire vineyards had been engulfed, killing plants that had been producing grapes for decades. Politicians in helicopters surveyed the inland ocean as it began to drain out to sea, leaving behind overturned cars in the middle of denuded fields, nearly six thousand families without homes, and a repair bill of more than a billion euros.

Eventually communications were restored and I was able to ring Meg Farrell at Cardet. The village is close to Anduze, which had borne the brunt of the inundation, receiving about 650 millimetres of rain in 24 hours. In itself, such a fall was tolerable, but the real threat came when the combined catchment surged down from the mountains, turning the river Gardon into an angry wall of water.

Meg had watched in disbelief as her street became a canal, the rising water level visible through glass panels by her front door. Soon the water poured in, filling the ground floor to a depth of three feet. Somehow she hoisted chairs and a sofa onto tabletops and carried Micheal's artwork upstairs. The upright piano was already safely ensconced on the first floor.

Other pianos fared worse. A friend of Meg's, who ran a rambling old stone guesthouse down the street, lost her prized concert grand. The invading water rose inexorably up the exquisitely tapered legs, filled the cracks between the hand-crafted ivory keys, and gently closed over the black polished lid, all in agonising slow motion.

'The place is devastated,' Meg told me. 'One man locked his two dogs in his car to keep them out of harm's way while he ran back indoors to try to rescue some valuables. When he came back, the car and the dogs were gone.'

Booker had better news. Much of his village was okay, although several people who had parked by the river lost their vehicles as the Vidourle scoured its banks clean on either side. The lower part of the Crumbs' basement had flooded. Having spent two months living on the town's low-water mark, I was grateful for the timing of my departure.

'There's a trench through the middle of the yard at the house in Uzès,' he said, 'but we got off lightly compared to the fellow with the plot of land next door. He'd only just ploughed it all up to start another sunflower crop. Now there's not an inch of topsoil left. Most of his livelihood is an organic soup on its way to the Mediterranean. It's sad back at the village, though. People are out searching up and down the river.'

'Are they trying to find their cars?'

'No – they've written off the cars. This is much worse. One of the swans is missing.'

The damage in the Vaucluse was not confined to the damp spots in my ceiling.

'Mate, this *vendange* is shit,' complained Matt, a week after the floods. 'Too much water, too late in the day. Half the fruit is splitting on the vine. We're just getting it out of the fields and into the vats as fast as we can to salvage whatever flavour might be left. Thank Christ it's going to end up on British supermarket shelves. For the guys trying to service the domestic market, it's a fuckin' catastrophe.'

The sun shone innocently on the bar. These days Gérard made my coffee the moment he saw me pass on my way to the *boulangerie*. Roberte was sellotaping some posters to the front doors. The word KARAOKE was written in large letters, the clarion call to a musical battle.

'The late summer concerts up at the château draw very good crowds,' she explained. (We suspected that her Deep Throat for château gossip was the gardener.) This was true; I had been to one of these chamber recitals. It took place in a magnificent drawing room lined with ancient tapestries, lit by candelabra that compounded the heat coming in from the open windows behind the performers. Schubert songs mingled with the sounds of cicadas outside and the rustle of people within, fanning themselves. It was no surprise the events were so popular.

Roberte outlined her strategy. 'We want to see some of those same people here at the Sports. This is our answer to the challenge from up the hill. It's Gérard's idea. Brilliant, yes? *Everyone* loves karaoke. The big night takes place next Saturday. So far we have twelve people coming. Will you be here?'

I glanced at my coffee, aware of a sense of obligation, but unable to rid myself of the doubt that those who had just savoured a recital of lieder by Schubert in a medieval château would want to let off steam afterwards in a smoky bar, listening to a stonemason's drunken wife wailing *I Will Always Love You.*

'*Bien sûr,*' I said. Matt was silent.

Later, we headed down to the wine co-operative behind the village so that I could see his vats.

Matt was adamant about the karaoke night. 'You can count me out, mate,' he decreed. 'My idea of hell is having a microphone shoved up my nose and then being forced to sing *My* fuckin' *Way.*'

'Ease up, big boy,' I countered. 'This is France. They'd probably make you have a crack at *La Mer.*'

'You can still forget it.' Charles Trenet could rest in peace.

The winery was a plain concrete building with none of the faux rusticity common to today's Cellar Doors. As we stepped into the entrance, a man hurried by, holding up a filthy rag to staunch blood streaming from the side of his head.

'They really put everything into making their wine,' I said diplomatically.

'Mate, I reckon nothing's changed much since the 50s. In Australia, a place like this would be closed down.'

Inside, the network of steel ladders and ramps resembled the interior of a particularly large submarine, except that all the liquid was on the inside. Matt opened a hatch, and a concentrated form of the yeasty smell I had noticed everywhere wafted out. He shone a torch into the blackness to show me the surface of a colourless, slowly bubbling primordial ooze.

'There you go,' he said. 'That's this year's shiraz.'

'Can I stick my head in for a better look?'

'I wouldn't recommend it. There's no oxygen in there – just the carbon dioxide you can see coming to the surface while it ferments. If you fell in, the gas would acidify your bloodstream. It'd all be over pretty quickly.'

'What a tragedy,' I lamented. 'To fall into a vat of fermenting wine, and then be denied the pleasure of drowning in it.'

The joint was not jumping when I arrived for the big karaoke night. None of the people looked as if they had come from the concert at the château. Most of them were children with painted faces. Some uncoiled streamers were draped over picture frames on the wall, and a mirrored ball hung desultorily from the middle of the ceiling.

'When are you expecting the visitors from up on the hill?' I asked Roberte, clinging to the present tense.

'This is all!' she replied brightly. 'With you, we now have thirteen.'

Her gardener boyfriend was the evening's DJ. He obviously relished his moments with the microphone, since they grew longer and louder with each announcement. So far, all of the children had been given the chance to parrot pop songs that had once motivated their mothers in discos. As the volume continued to be pumped up, echoes of Hot Chocolate's early 80s song *It Started With A Kiss* slapped off the front of houses facing the *place* before racing uphill to the open windows of the château. This would give Schubert a run for his money.

Roberte introduced me to her boyfriend. He shook my hand and spoke in staccato bursts.

'It's good that you're here. Quite a night, eh? Don't worry; it's all arranged. You're on next.'

'*Pardon?*' Matt's description of hell roared back into my memory.

'Roberte told us all about your interest in music. We decided that you should show us all how it's done.'

Somewhere at the bottom of this travesty on the make was some botched French in a previous conversation. The error could only have been mine.

'Well, I don't really have anything prepared. Perhaps I . . .'

'Hey! It's karaoke! You don't have to prepare. Everything is provided – except that voice of yours, of course. We're all very excited.'

He grabbed his microphone.

'Your attention, everyone! We are very happy to have our friend from so far away who has come to sing for us tonight. I hope you will give a big Bar des Sports welcome to Mister Chris, and one of the most celebrated songs of all time. This is it . . . MY WAY!'

He handed me the mike and activated an orchestra by punching a button on his machine with an outsized gesture. The lyric appeared on a screen to my left, while the mirrored ball started to turn overhead. Somebody turned the sound up even higher. Whatever I did now would sound like an air-raid siren.

'GO, MISTER CHRIS!' yelled Gérard, as if he were at a football match.

'Thank you, ladies and gentlemen,' I said in English, and indeed, those few words were the most successful part of my performance. The hushed valediction of the first few lines was delivered Rex Harrison style, without actually singing, but at

When I bit off more than I could chew

life began to imitate art when I recognised my incapacity to capture the song's full emotional range. Therefore, by

I ate it up and spit it out

I sidestepped the opportunity for the 'big moment', resorting to a type of scat singing that sat oddly with the increasingly monumental accompaniment. Snapping my fingers on the offbeat didn't help.

The volume must have been deafening outside. At the penultimate line

The record shows I took the blows

the first consonant on 'blows' set off a car alarm in the *place*. Undeterred by this intrusive descant, I bent my knees, closed my eyes, threw my head back and emoted the knockout ending as best I could, sustaining the last note

Wa-a-a-a-a-a-a-a-y!!!

while the electronic band thundered to a triumphant close. As the echo of the final chord rippled down the valley, several dogs howled.

Unfortunately, a crisis prevented the audience from showing the full extent of its approval. A child choked on a pretzel and was carried out, upside down and screaming. The gardener looked puzzled.

On a scale of courage, I felt my rendition ranked up there with the four-foot leap at Roquevaire. But more important was the extent to which this achievement might have pushed me towards the overarching goal of my trip. Had I *swung*? I did not know how to ask this in French, so probed instead for swing's principal telltale sign.

'Tell me, Gérard – my singing makes you want to tap your feet?'

Later I realised I had probably said 'touch your toes', which explained his momentary look of confusion. Then his forehead relaxed, as he finally comprehended my meaning.

'*Non*, Chris,' he replied. 'I scratched my arse, though.'

My path to swing still had some way to go.

TEN

SWING IS THE THING

VALAIDA, 'QUEEN OF THE TRUMPET', WITH SWING
ACCOMPANIMENT, LONDON, 1937

The trumpets are blowin'
They know the sound
The music is goin'
Around and around

WEEKS FLEW BY (or did they *crawl*? – with time on
my hands, it felt the same) and autumn's melancholy
dress sense was forced on everything that couldn't walk. Cold,
merciless rain skeletonised the vines and cowed the clumps of
trimmed lavender. Stargazing with a foot in the pool became
a memory. Up in the village, Roberte unfolded the glass front
doors of the Bar des Sports to seal out the chill.

Being the temporary châtelain of the hillside, I felt a
paternalistic need to protect all of the creatures that shared it
with me, particularly when the hunting season began. One
morning I stumbled across several men with guns at the foot
of the hill. They wore thick boots and military fatigues.

'*Bonjour*,' I said suspiciously, 'What are you all doing here?'

'*Sanglier*,' one of them remarked sourly, pointing at churned earth between rows of vines. 'We're following some tracks. Have you seen it?'

I resented this gauche show of arms so close to my front door almost as much as any inconvenience that might be visited upon the pig, and did not wish to feel complicit in the inevitable blowing out of its brains. For a moment, I thought of pointing in the opposite direction and telling the stalkers that it went that-a-way. Instead, I opted for innocent jocularity.

'*Non*,' I shrugged. 'What did it do – rob a bank?' The quip went down almost as well as *My Way*.

At least my lizards were safe inside the protective crook of the courtyard. Theirs was a relationship that I overheard, but never observed directly, like the night of love through an open window in Booker's village so long ago. The first lizard lived among the leaves of the vine under the bedroom windowsill. He announced himself shortly after my arrival, rasping his way through the hot summer days.

After a few weeks of solo riffs, another rasp began in the vine on the opposite wall of the courtyard. This became a conversation, perhaps an invitation, for the second rasp began making its way through the network of branches around the perimeter of the courtyard in the direction of the first. It could have been the prelude to a winner-takes-all territorial dispute, but I preferred to think of it as a courtship; that they were zeroing in on each other in the reptilian equivalent of lovers reuniting on a beach in French films. This was the only true romance of my adventure so far, and I wanted it to work.

'Have you actually *seen* them?' Matt asked me one evening. We were sipping wine in the courtyard as a farewell. His job done, with a serviceable Côte de Lubéron soon to be extracted from the vats, he would be returning to Australia in a couple of days.

'No. But I bet they're cute.'

'*Cute*? By now, one of them is probably eating the other's head.'

'No way, buddy. Right now, there's some cold-blooded *lerv* happening up there.' (This was, admittedly, our second bottle.) 'Get it on, you guys. Get it *on*.' At my own cue, I jumped up and improvised a lizard love dance on the chilly flagstones. 'Get it on, *yeah*,' I sang.

Matt was incredulous. 'Mate . . . has anyone told you that you need to get *out* more?'

He doesn't understand, I thought disparagingly (and drunkenly). We're talking about my *friends* here. For this is what happens when you spend time watching the passage of the seasons on a hillside from a farmhouse window: you become inordinately fond of invisible lizards. And not just lizards, but all of those things you had previously never stopped to look at or sniff: the shape of the olive tree nearest the pool, the colour of the grass on the farther side of the clearing, the fragrance of a certain bloom on the climbing rose. What surprised me was not the lode of sentimentality in my character underlying all this – almost everyone wants to hug a tree sooner or later – but the *particularity* of my passions. This – dare I say it? – love of my surroundings, instead of blinding me, was making me more observant. I was *noticing* so many small things in the world around me with the same attention to detail that I had hitherto lavished upon music or, more ineffectively, upon myself. Looking outward with care was therefore as much a relief as a source of new pleasure.

My American real estate friend took me to a dinner in Menerbes, hosted by a wealthy Texan heiress who owned the biggest place in the village. She imported her chef from the US and installed him in his own house down the street. He cooked so superbly that at the end of our dinner for twelve, he was summoned to the dining room to be applauded. But the casual opulence! Floor to ceiling shelves in two huge reception rooms filled with thousands of books; beautiful ornaments arrayed on antique wooden tables. It was impossible to decide what to look at first.

'She has a lot of stuff in there,' I commented to my friend in her car afterwards. 'How much time does she spend in Menerbes?'

'About three months a year.'

'I don't get it,' I said. 'How does she have enough time to *notice* everything?'

On Christmas Eve I drove up to Ansouis for an evening drink. The village was still, wrapped in the hush that presages astonishing events. Strands of coloured lights flickered in mute celebration on the *place* des Hôtes. A Christmas tree stood dolefully at the entrance to the car park.

The next day I would be lunching with *la famille* Booker. Tonight, though, was mine, and I intended to hear the late Mass in the church of the nearby village of Cucuron. It would be said in the old Provençal language, and there was to be a Blessing of the Lambs before (one assumed) they were turned into Christmas Day *gigots*.

The Bar des Sports was still open. Gérard and Roberte looked surprised when I walked in, for I was rarely anything other than a morning visitor. What, they asked, was I doing this evening?

'Well, I'm having a private celebration for myself,' I replied. 'You see, it's my birthday.'

Mouths fell open. 'But you did not tell us this morning,' said Roberte. She put down the broom with which she had been sweeping the floor prior to closing, and turned to the last customers at the bar. 'Did you hear that, boys? Our friend is having his birthday! *Bon anniversaire!*'

Patrick and Maurice were obviously at the wrong end of a big afternoon at the bar. They lifted their glasses in a show of emotion, and congratulated me with handshakes of tight-gripped sincerity. No sooner was this done than Maurice excused himself and hurried out the door.

'Don't worry about Maurice,' explained Gérard. 'His wife hates him coming to the bar. She thinks he makes a fool of himself when he's completely *soûl*. She's right, so he goes home every hour to placate her. We'll have locked up by the time he gets back.'

I raised my glass in another toast. 'To all of us, and the Bar des Sports. Sadly, my friends, I have to leave the day after tomorrow.'

Roberte and Gérard's protestations were cut short by the reappearance of Maurice, standing in the rectangle of light outside the closed doors. Something glimmered in his hands. He was holding a trumpet.

'I hope his wife doesn't hear about this,' warned Roberte.

Maurice disappeared from view. Within seconds, a strangulated sound emerged from under the village Christmas tree. Fragments of a familiar melody could be detected amid the welter of split notes: *Happy Birthday To You*. After playing it once, he attempted a second jazzier version that tottered for a few bars before collapsing in a puddle of cacophony and spoken asides. Dogs howled again down the valley.

Windows opened across the street. 'Maurice, is it you playing that bloody trumpet?' someone yelled. 'Don't you know it's Christmas?'

'There's a birthday party at the Sports,' Maurice slurred loudly. 'Everyone's invited!'

'Great!' said some Americans, who had emerged from their nearby holiday *gîte* to check out the racket.

Corinne the *boulanger*'s wife passed by with two of her children on their way home to unwrap presents. 'What's going on?' she asked. Monsieur Rossignol, who lived just next door to Bruno's *agence de presse*, called back to her as he burst through the bar doors. 'Something about an important gathering at the Sports. Sounds like we should be here. We can go to Mass afterwards.'

Drawn by curiosity and the bizarre siren song from the tree, about twenty people came in, calling for Christmas drinks. Maurice followed, red-faced and triumphant, clutching his trumpet. He raised it to his lips, but was dissuaded from playing any further by having extra beers pressed upon him. Everybody shook my hand as Roberte finally revealed the identity of the stranger who had been such a reticent morning fixture at the bar these past few months, apart from his surprising performance of *My Way*. This spontaneous gathering was already bigger than the karaoke night. 'It's a good party, isn't it?' said Bruno, ruddier than usual.

'Ah *oui*, Bruno,' I replied. '*Chaud.*'

Filling quickly with Christmas and other spirits, I felt the first pre-emptive waves of nostalgia. Or was it nausea? Both words now sounded the same when I pronounced them. I needed some pretzels.

'I'll be back,' I assured those who expressed a polite regret at my imminent departure. But did one ever have the same adventure twice, or simply resume the story after the last exciting episode? I would miss having a Zorro around to open the doors to women's apartments, but you can't have everything. And it was time to jump. 'I'll be back!' I declared – actually, it was more like 'I am coming here again!' – making a grand exit for the Provençal Mass in Cucuron while trumpet flourishes and shouts of *bon anniversaire* rang around the room.

I heard later that the party wound up soon after my departure. Maurice's wife was appalled by the affair and refused to let him in when he came home. He spent the night before Christmas in the bar, curled up with his trumpet under the counter.

I went back, of course. It was only a few months later, but time enough for sadness to be introduced into my adventure.

Micheal Farrell finally succumbed to his illness at home in Cardet. The village mourned and gave Meg a commemorative plaque that now sits in their vegetable patch.

Less expected was the death of the pizza restaurant owner from Booker's village. One night after closing, he had drunkenly started a more violent altercation than usual with his wife that culminated in his driving out of town in the middle of a heavy rainstorm. His wrecked vehicle was found several kilometres up the road. He appeared to have hit a pig.

One day a cardboard tube arrived in the mail from France. Inside was a poster that read:

> You are invited to a
> **SYMPHONY OF CURRY AND SWING**
> featuring
> **TOM BAKER**
> and other jazz luminaries
> Pianist and Sommelier
> Booker T.

Such an announcement merited a long distance phone call.

'Hey! It's a party,' said Booker down the line. 'Tom's coming through between gigs in Biarritz and Holland, and he's bringing some crack American players with him. You can't let an opportunity like this pass when there are so many good musos together in the one place. I haven't had a good summertime piss-up for a couple of years, and this one shows every sign of being steamy. I dare say that *your senses will never be the same.*'

'But there's no mention of the time, place or date.'

'We're after a select group. The Crumbs can't make it, but Pete and Nini are coming. So is the local women's kick boxing champion, who promises to bring along several carloads of nurses and speech therapists.'

I mentioned the fatal car accident involving the pizza cook.

'Given the guy's continual state of inebriation, such an end wasn't altogether a surprise,' he remarked. 'It must have been quite a pig.'

'Never mind the pig,' I interrupted. 'What happened to the wife?'

'She's never looked better. Monique at the salon gave her a complete makeover, and I must say she scrubs up a real vixen. Business at the restaurant is booming because every available man in the area is trying to woo her. She went and bought herself a Harley-Davidson with the extra profits.'

It may be a distinctly middle-aged thing to prefer the known to the unknown, or perhaps my adventure resembled a symphony arriving at its final recapitulation, like the end of Tchaikovsky's Fifth, with trumpets in a sunny major key. Either might have explained my feeling of well-being at the now-familiar sights outside the windows of Booker's Kangoo: zooming into Uzès, tilting through his front gate in a precision move, squinting in the hard noonday sunlight, and waving to the neighbours on the top floors of the big building across the road. A trumpet was blazing away on the Kangoo's sound system, but this was not Tchaikovsky.

The track had begun with a woman's voice, husky and sassy: *Swing Is The Thing*.

'She sounds like a *Louise* Armstrong,' I said. 'Who is it?'

'Her name is Valaida Snow, a major entertainer in both the United States and Europe during the 30s. She came a cropper when the war broke out. At the time she was living in Denmark, and the Nazis interned her until she could be repatriated. It can't have been pleasant. Some writers say that she never got over it.'

'And the trumpeter?'

'That, too, is Valaida. In her time, she was dubbed "Queen

of the Trumpet". But her dominion expanded to include the violin, cello, accordion, harp and clarinet. I've probably left a few out. In fact, the only multi-instrumentalist I can think of who is in that league is our dear friend Tom Baker, who differs from Valaida in playing all of his instruments with complete virtuosity. Valaida eventually concentrated on the trumpet. Your Armstrong analogy, while perceptive, is not original. Back in the 30s she was often billed as "Little Louis". She had musical sisters whose names testify to their mother's liking for a good sound – Lavaida and Alvaida.'

Tom was a very good reason for coming all the way back to France. He would be the star turn of this advertised 'symphony', providing the swing *and* the curry. Based in Australia and considered one of the best heritage jazz players on the international scene, he spent a large portion of each year appearing in festivals on both sides of the Atlantic, playing one or all of a flotilla of instruments: trumpet, trombone, tuba, baritone and alto sax, various clarinets, string bass and accordion. Booker had often played piano with him, and they were to be supported for this exclusive front lawn gig by an elite group of American jazz players. The music was going to be *hot*.

So was the food. Tom was as adept with culinary ingredients as he was with musical ones; in particular the spices, powders, herbs and pastes of Indian cooking. I had enjoyed his aromatic mélange of food and music several times back in

Sydney, moving from *balti* to Bix Beiderbecke, served on a variety of platters. For this party, he offered to prepare enough curries for forty people. Booker's prediction of the night's impact was right – this would be an extravaganza for those with tongues, noses and ears. The eyes, I felt, could look after themselves.

We convened in Booker's studio over kirs and the Dorsey brothers to discuss the order of events.

'Right,' he said. 'The boys arrive in three days. I've found a newly built *gîte* about fifteen minutes away from here. The showerheads were being installed when they confirmed the reservation this morning. It looks like we are about thirty-seven in number, so I've told the kickboxer that she can circulate the word to every nurse she knows.'

'She'll be good to have around if a fight breaks out.'

'I rather suspect the nurses won't be fighting over us, although I have been endeavouring to cut back on Domaine Houtier of late in pursuit of a more svelte figure. So, that leaves the issue of food. Tom's already given me a list. And therein lies the problem.'

'What problem? You have an amazing amateur chef coming to cook curry for you, and this is France. It's *full* of food.'

'Precisely the point. *This is France.* Gastronomic centre of the universe it may be, but its regional cuisine is based on what comes directly out of what the French call their *terroir*. This is still a mono-cultural – one could almost say a parochial – society in matters of the table. Half of North Africa lives around here, so it's a pity we didn't decide to go Moroccan. But India is not next door. I suppose some of the French have met a curry at some point, but it isn't the sort of dish they would choose to take home to their mother. For Tom to make a curry he'll need the right ingredients. You won't find them in the supermarkets – I've looked, believe me – and there isn't a curry shop between here and Paris. *That* is the problem. I don't know why I didn't think of it when Tom made the suggestion.'

'Have you tried the Uzès market?'

Booker sighed. 'I suppose we could. But I *hate* the Uzès market. It's always full of people haggling in Dutch.'

It was a Tuesday, and the next big market did not take place until Thursday, just before the musicians and their chef were due to arrive. If curry powders could not be found among the phalanx of produce, fabrics and tourists, Saturday's party would feature a less exotic symphony of *fromage*.

Our first search of the crowded market square yielded nothing. In quiet desperation, Booker asked one of the veteran stallholders if she knew of such an unusual thing as a curry powder vendor.

'But yes! You're after Alice,' she said. 'She only comes once every few weeks, depending on how much she has to sell. It looks like . . . *voilà!* She is over there, near the arcade.'

Alice turned out to be a housewife from Avignon with no obvious Indian genetic heritage. She was coy about her suppliers, saying only that everything was carefully stored in her garage, a pungent suburban grotto in which she secretively concocted her powders. Before her was a bounty rare in this part of the world; jars of pastes and large earthenware bowls displayed on a long, cloth-covered bench, their contents iridescent in the morning sun – red, yellow, burnt orange, light brown.

'The colours remind me of an autumnal pig-infested vine field over in Provence,' I remarked. 'This is what he wanted?'

Booker was checking off a hand-written list. 'Let me see . . . garam masala, cardamom, medium and hot curry powders, extra turmeric, shrimp paste . . . yes, no, yes. It's not all here, but we'll fill in the gaps with chilli. Done! . . . I hope.'

'Yo, *trashman*,' boomed Tom, his native Californian drawl overlayed intriguingly by a newer Australian one, when the van carrying him and the others rolled into chez Booker later that afternoon after they had checked into their *gîte*. The long drive across from Biarritz had been a warm one. Tom's broad, knobbly featured face was florid, his luxuriant thatch of hair plastered in sweat. And this was *before* the curry.

'How's the place?' asked Booker.

'Not bad, dad. Some of the showerheads keep falling off, but they say it'll be fixed by tonight. You got the stuff?'

The back of the Kangoo was opened and Tom surveyed the stash. Lids were prised off plastic containers, potions sniffed, moistened fingers dipped into powders. In this heat, it felt like going through customs control on the Mexican border.

'Not bad,' he said. 'Not too good, either. But we can ginger some of this up – with more ginger, for instance. Curry takes time to make if it's gonna be good, so we'll have to start tonight.'

Books of this kind frequently include souvenir recipes, so that the reader can reproduce something from the location being described without having to stump up the cash for a plane ticket. Sadly, during our two-day marathon cook-up I saw no recipe anywhere. Experience and a great cook's sublime alchemical intuition must have stamped a template inside Tom's rather large cranium. This much I perceived: one builds the eventual flavour of a good curry in layers, tasting and adjusting, tasting again, sending in small quotas of extra spice like riot police to curb any lurches towards the incendiary, the sweet or the bland. Colour is also an issue, and in this Tom turned his pans into palettes, tinting with turmeric like Tintoretto.

Curry and jazz go well together because they are created the same way. You know what you want to make and the basic system for getting there, and rely on improvisation and a quick response to the emerging chemistry to make the trip. A *recipe*? It would be just as effective as a colour-by-numbers pattern for the *Mona Lisa*.

Cooking for forty people is an industrial exercise, so we formed a dedicated production line of peelers, choppers, stirrers and *plongeurs* to support the master artist at his easel, bending over his work in progress to lick the brush. Meanwhile, Booker and the others counterpointed the *tok!* of knives on wooden boards, sounds of sizzling saucepans and Tom's equally sizzling imprecations with some swingin' *Nachtmusik* from the adjacent dining room. We all retired at five o'clock each morning, musicians and kitchen hands alike pleased with the way things were cooking.

'Hey, *amigo!* Are you still jumping?'

Pete and Nini were among the first to arrive. His hair was longer and curled halfway down the back of his neck in this year's look for Mexican outlaws. Nini was as finely packaged as ever in the sheer leopard skin-patterned tights that had first excited the Crumbs' friend, Gary. She was soon involved in a broken English conversation with Joel, the visiting bass player, whose attention never really returned to the music for the rest of the night.

A man walked in wearing pyjamas and a cowboy hat.

'*Bonsoir*,' he said brightly to Booker. 'I am Wyatt Earp.'

Booker was immediately suspicious. 'Are you from across the road?'

'*Non*,' the visitor answered indignantly. 'I come from Dodge City.'

'Mother!' Booker called. 'Would you give Mr Earp a champagne? I have to make a phone call.'

Tables were set up on the lawn, and people moved downstairs to serve themselves from large steaming pots before finding an accommodating pool of light among the jumble of house lamps. Booker's upright had been carted outside to the tiled landing near the front door. The band set itself up around him and the Symphony began, melodies and aromas floating into a sky now pierced by stars.

It was a night for epiphanies. As I joined the line waiting for the food, a young man clutching his plate of chicken korma made his way to me through the crush.

'Hi,' he said. 'We never met, and I gather you stayed in Booker's village for a while. I live there too, up on the hill. My name's Ian.'

'Good to meet you, Ian,' I replied. '*Ian* . . . for some reason, your name rings a bell. Somebody must have mentioned you to me. What do you do there?'

'I play the violin . . . well, to be more accurate, I'm a fiddler. I play folk music.'

My mouth fell open. *The Folks Who Live On The Hill. Be Zorro.*

'That's astonishing,' I said.

'Why?'

'Because in a funny way you were the most significant person in my life during my stay. For one magic moment there, you almost carried me.'

Ian was understandably perplexed by this confession.

'Wow – but when did I . . .'

'*Bonsoir, mon ténor.*'

The singing voice might have been a soprano, but the speaking voice was a rich alto. I turned around to face the Maestro.

Her face seemed less lined, more relaxed, and the subtly encroaching greyness in her hair looked almost aristocratic. The self-effacing, contour-blurring mode of dress from the previous summer had been exchanged for something that paid her figure the compliment it deserved: a crimson bodice with a bright floral skirt. Tonight, nobody would have to wait for the upbeat.

'*Chef,*' I exclaimed. 'How . . . how is the *Joli Jeu*?'

'Oh, I don't conduct them any more,' she said. 'The choir broke up.' So there would be no more downbeats, either.

This was the second surprise for me in as many minutes. 'What happened?'

Her smile dimmed, but only slightly. 'Let's just say that the tenor section proved to be unreliable.'

We heaped beef vindaloo and curried whole eggs onto plates and wandered through lamplight and starlight for a place to eat. The shouts and laughter that had been the soundtrack for the opening drinks subsided into a measured murmur as curry took centre stage. The band obliged the circumstances by taking it cool and slow. Only when plates were gathered up an hour later, and more wine was opened, did swing become the thing. Tom's trumpet cooed and brayed, signalling the start of the dancing.

I scurried over to Booker, noticing that his glass of *rouge* was empty. Not for the first time that evening, the band was playing without their bass.

'Where's Joel?' I asked.

'Walking around red-eyed and increasingly incoherent,' he half-shouted over the blare of brass, his left hand still pounding a rhythm. 'He keeps going around the side of the house with Nini for one of her "special" cigarettes. You know what they say about women in leopard skin – they always show their spots.'

Symphonies require a grand finale. How good it would have been to say that this summer night was one of frantic loose-limbed carousing that the police were summoned to break up at dawn! Alas, the relaxing effects of the warm air and a surfeit of wine and curry overcame the blandishments of the few up-tempo numbers the band could manage without half of their rhythm section. Even now I could see Joel, wreathed in smoke, wandering with Nini up and down Booker's drive. The highest point came when Pete climbed the thirty-foot tree that dominated the front lawn.

Instead of a general hubbub, the party became a chain of small intimacies. Couples danced slowly, deep in conversation, as Tom exchanged his trumpet for a more languid trombone. The band lost its pianist when Booker, abandoning all worries about thresholds for the evening, deserted his place to be noticed by a nurse near a tall hedge.

I asked the Maestro to dance. Since we were both carrying sizeable amounts of vindaloo, we swayed at a moderate tempo.

'You know, *chef*,' I mused, 'I took great pleasure in our conducting lessons.'

The former equestrian rubbed the back of my head, as if I were a Shetland pony. '*Moi aussi*,' she said.

Sheriffs came to escort Wyatt Earp back to Dodge City, breaking up a conversation he was enjoying with Norma. She raised her scotch in farewell as he was led away. 'It was *very* kind of you to come,' she said with impeccable gentility. 'You will come back and see us again soon, won't you?'

Several glasses of red wine later, I sat in a plastic chair under the big tree with my face turned to the sky. This was one of those nights that Shakespeare raved about in *The Merchant of Venice*. And didn't Alan Jay Lerner write something about a *Wand'rin' Star*? I could discern how fast the stars were wandering by noticing the change in their positions through the branches. Booker was back at the keyboard, idling slow chords while Tom poured a final blue note into the night. This Symphony was over.

Those stars wander slowly, I thought. Why shouldn't they? They have all the time in the world. Beyond the world, even. I sipped my wine again, noticing the slight sense of spin this induced. It was good to be a mere mortal with a lifespan shorter than the blink of an eye. Imagine how interminable middle age would be if you were a star.

Then I saw all of us going around and around on our piece of spinning shellac, and felt rhythms pulsing everywhere: the stars, the passing of a season, the soft thrum of a left hand striding on a keyboard, my own breathing. Straining to hear their articulation, I gradually became aware of another base rhythm underlying it all, played by a faraway brass section:

Doo-wah doo-wah, doo-wah doo-wah,
doo-wah doo-wah, doo . . .

'*Hey.*' Jolted out of my reverie, I saw Tom standing next to my chair.

'Hi, Tom. Everything was great tonight. When did the music stop?'

'Just a moment ago. We didn't have to play any more. You were obviously having a great time without us.'

'What do you mean?' I said, puzzled. 'I'm just unwinding.'

'I could see you sitting over here, looking up and tapping your feet.' Tom's sly grin was just noticeable in the lamplight. 'Man, you were *swinging.*'

GLOSSARY OF MUSICAL TERMS

Swing (i) (with apologies to *The Grove Dictionary of Music and Musicians*)

A quality in jazz performance resulting from the conflict between a fixed pulse and the wide variety of accent and rubato that the musician plays against it. The precise point of difference at which swing occurs is unquantifiable, even on the scale of quantum mechanics, but is felt naturally by certain musicians who are then able to transmit the sensation to their listeners. White middle-aged males are insensate to swing unless they are 1. genetically modified, 2. able to play a musical instrument, or 3. drunk. In jazz, the first quality often connotes the other two.

Swing (ii)

The name given to a jazz style and a related phase of popular music that originated around 1930 when New Orleans jazz was in decline.

Symphony

(Fr. *simphonie, symphonie*; Ger. *Sinfonie, Symphonie*; It. *sinfonia*)

The period in an orchestral concert when husbands of certain audience members are most likely to look at their watches.

These excursions for large instrumental ensembles were models of concision until Beethoven decided to turn the symphony into a metaphor for life with a time span to match. Symphonies became more tear-stained with Tchaikovsky, interminable with Bruckner, and Freudian with Mahler. Richard Strauss removed the metaphysics and made the symphony into happy snaps depicting a day on a mountain (*Eine Alpensinfonie*) and a night with the wife (*Symphonia domestica*). Diana Ross and the Supremes claimed to hear one whenever their boyfriends were nearby (decades before the invention of the iPod), while English rock group The Verve, reverting to the Mahlerian prototype, described 'this life' as a 'bittersweet symphony' in the 1997 album *Urban Hymns*. Unable to swing their way out of this dualism, the group promptly split up.

SONG CREDITS

Frenesi	(Dominguez/Charles/Russell)
Women Will Rule The World	(Quevedo)
I'll Take The South	(Klages/Palmer)
Avant de mourir	(Boulanger)
Night and Day	(Porter)
The Folks Who Live On The Hill	(Kern/Hammerstein II)
Junk Man	(Loesser/Meyer)
Brise Napolitaine	(Vetese/Peyronnin)
Keep Your Undershirt On	(Kalmar/Ruby)
Get Out And Get Under The Moon	(Tobias/Jerome/Shay)
Caravan	(Ellington/Tizol)
Time On My Hands	(Youmans/Gordon/ Adamson)
Swing Is The Thing	(Mercer)